Having Sex W

MW01195097

Joe Holman

Dedication

I joyfully dedicate this book to my BFF. Denise, you and I grew up together. We have been best friends since 1980 and love buddies since 1984. You are my role model of friendship and life. Thanks for being such a good friend and for all the great sex!

Table of Contents

Forward

"It will never last."

"Too young to be married."

"I bet she is pregnant."

"She will regret it."

"She is making a big mistake."

"She needs to live life before she gets married."

These are just some of the many things said about my beautiful wife. The people who said them all realized, decades ago, they were wrong. Denise and I were high school sweethearts. I was an old, mature and wise high school senior. Well, I thought I was all that and a bag of chips. The truth is, I was a below average 17-year-old kid. Denise was a few months into her 14th year when we went on our first date. Fast forward a couple of years and I am in college. Denise is now a junior in high school. I received the blessing of both of our parents and asked her to marry me. She was not yet 17 years old, yet engaged to be married. We followed the advice of our parents and did not get married until she finished High School. She was engaged for half of her junior year and all of her senior. She graduated in May, turned 18 in June and we were married in July. We jokingly say she was 17 years and 13 months when we got married.

People do not expect a marriage to last in our culture. It depends on which study you read, but virtually all of them put the divorce rate over 40% and many state it is over 50%. Divorce hits virtually every family, directly or indirectly. That is a normal situation. How in the world can a marriage last when it was little more than a high school crush sealed with a ring and a ceremony? Surely, one or both of the people will grow up and out of love. They will soon realize their high school crush was just hormonal infatuation and regret it.

We wed on July 21, 1984. Since the beginning of our lives together, we have grown more in love. I love her, and she loves me, more today than at any point in history. Our love is deeper, more mature, wise, and passionate. We have lived our lives together and are both better because of it. Love has grown through the victories and the challenges of our lives. Our love grew with the birth of each child and with the death of my oldest son. I office in our home and she homeschools the children. This means we are together all the time. Yet, we do not get on each other's nerves. I tell people in marriage counseling, "I would rather be with my wife doing nothing than doing anything with anyone else in the world. Being bored with her is better than excitement with another."

How?

How can we be more passionately in love now than ever?

How can our love story continue to be written?

How can we be closer today than yesterday?

What is the secret?

That is the purpose of this book. We are better today than ever before because we are best friends and have great sex. If I could summarize the joy of marriage in a simple sentence, it is the title of this book. "Having Sex With My Best Friend."

The book will have a little bit of an introduction to give branches for the fruit, and then there are two main sections.

The first one is to be best friends. The second one, and men, please read it after you read the first one…no cheating…the second one is on the importance of frequent and great sex. I believe this is the actual order. Great sex results from a great relationship, and then the sex improves the relationship which improves the sex which improves…you get it.

My desire for you is to encourage your marriage in both arenas. I want you to be married to your best friend, even if at the beginning of the book you are not. I also want the rest of your sex life to be the best of your sex life.

God's Will

"We committed to the marriage. We will not get a divorce. It is God's will that we do not get a divorce." Shelly said to me in counseling as her husband, sitting in a chair he moved a few more inches away from her as they sat down, nodded. "God doesn't want us to get a divorce." Over and over, they both emphasized God's will. No divorce. They believed if they did not get a divorce, they were doing God's will.

Shelly and her husband echoed what so many other Christian couples said to me over the years. Something has happened to our goals for marriage. I said something which shocked them. I have said it too many times to many others.

I spoke. "I disagree. That is not God's will. You said it was His will for you to not get a divorce. That is not true."

Generally, at this point, they give me their attention. Maybe they think I am giving them a glimmer of hope. They hate their marriage and want a divorce. They wished it would end. The problem is they are Christians, and it is God's will for them to 'not' get a divorce. Was I giving them a 'Get Out of Jail Free' card?

I continue. "I applaud you for seeking to follow God's will in your marriage. That is the key. However, you are shortchanging His will for you. God's will is so much more than 'no divorce'. He wills, desires, and wants you to have an incredible marriage! God wants you to be passionately in love with each other! Our Lord wants you to enjoy your lives together. He wants you to have a marriage packed full of love, joy, hope, peace, forgiveness, kindness, gentleness, respect, honor, patience and great sex. He wants your lives to be an illustration of the love Jesus has for the church. God wants to restore and redeem your marriage. He wants it to be a role model for all who know you. He wants to point to you and declare the awesomeness of your relationship to the angels. His will is for your marriage relationship, the way you love and show your love to each other, to glorify Him. Don't settle for 'no divorce.' If you had the choice of living the next thirty years of your life in a hospital bed connected to machines unable to leave it, or to have a life of adventure and service, would you say, 'God doesn't want me to die' and then crawl into a bed and be miserable?"

I continued, "Does God want you to 'not die' or does He desire you to have an abundant life?

Does God want you to 'not be defeated' or does He want you to be 'more than a conqueror'?

Does God will for you to 'not hate' or does He desire for you to love others?

I can, with absolute confidence, tell you God desires far more for your marriage than for you to not be divorced! You need to as well!"

I raise my voice a tad and get a little excited as I drive this home. God gave us a floor and a ceiling. The floor is do not get divorced. The ceiling is the heavens and a relationship which brings joy to us and honor to the Lord. We made the floor the goal. We reach the floor and then live on it like pigs wallowing in the muck and mud, even though above us is a high rise of joy. I know Christian couples who live in different bedrooms. Just this week, I discovered my daughter has a friend whose parents live in different houses on the same property. The husband lives in the apartment over the garage and the wife lives in the house. They committed to 'no divorce'. However, they do not want to be around each other, so they live in totally different places. The amazing thing is they both feel as if God is pleased with them for not divorcing. God wants so much more for your marriage than you do. Start desiring His will for your life!

"We don't fight. We pretty much never argue about anything. The truth is, our marriage is simply a business." Laura, a homeschooling mom of two, told me when she and her husband came for counseling. She continued. "We have been married for 9 years. We know what it takes to manage the household and we do the tasks. We don't have his/her jobs. We both work together and get it all done quite efficiently. We make it to all the children's activities. We both serve at church. The laundry is done, and the house is clean. We are good business partners. Yet, we both want more than we have. Our relationship is not bad, but it is not good either."

This goes along with the error of God's will equating no divorce. We also think if we do not fight or argue, we are happy. Happiness is not the automatic result of not being angry. An uneasy ceasefire is not peace. Peace is far more than the absence of conflict. Peace is a force which conquers conflict. Yet, I think Laura and her husband are the example of the vast majority of evangelical Christian marriages. We don't fight. We get things done. We are pretending to be happy. Since we are not 'unhappy', we must be happy. It just doesn't feel like it.

Our homes are efficient businesses staffed by unhappy employees who do their job and hate their cubicle. We do it. We get it done. The tasks are all checked off. We do our tasks but are dissatisfied with our job. Our homes and marriages are an endless cycle of to-do task lists, and our communication becomes an inter-office memo assigning the week's responsibilities. Many times, the product of our business becomes our children. We shift our relationship from that of a wife and husband to a set of parents. I am a father more than a husband. We focus on the myriads of needs the children bring us. It exhausts us. We do not have the energy for each other. This happens starting at birth and by the time the oldest is three, our lives unintentionally morphed into parental units solving problems. We are not husband and wife. We are dad and mom.

I can speak from personal experience. In 1994, I pastored a church plant in Colorado. Our fourth child was on the way. In my mind, things were going well. The church was successful. Folks were coming to Christ. Denise was a great mom and pastor's wife with plenty of her own ministry opportunities. Everything ran efficiently. I came home one day, and Denise said she needed to talk.

"I want you to know that I love you and always will." She started. I could tell this was serious. She took a breath and said, "I am committed to you and Christ. No matter what. We will get through it. However, I must know. Are you having an affair?"

It shocked me. I moved from being flabbergasted to angry. I could not believe she even thought it. I started listing off all the tasks I did at home. I talked about how much I helped her manage the house and did laundry, dishes, change diapers, feed children, etc.

She answered. "I did not say you don't do chores. The point is your heart is not here. When you are home, you want to be somewhere else. When you are somewhere else, you don't want to be home. All we are to you is something else on your to-do list."

The Holy Spirit brought Malachi to my mind. He prophesied of John the Baptist and one function John would do to prepare folks for the Kingdom of God and the Messiah. It is the last verse in the Old Testament.

"He will turn the hearts of the fathers back to their children and the hearts of the children to their fathers." (Malachi 4.6a)

The Holy Spirit used her to speak His truth to me. My heart and passion for my family was gone. I did my duty, but without joy. I had no passion for my family. I was present in body but absent in heart.

My story repeats every day across the country. Houses are full of moral, Bible believing, no-fighting, passionateness couples doing the business of marriage. We even stress the work aspect of it. "Work" at your marriage. Put in the "work" needed in your relationship. Anniversary posts on social media say, "It hasn't been easy, and we had our tough times. But we are committed to each other. Happy Anniversary!" In other words, "I am stuck in this relationship." Let me ask you, when you were dating and in the first few months of your marriage, how much "work" did it take to enjoy being with each other?

Even sex and lovemaking become a business. It is not lovemaking. It is quickie sex. How many times do you have sex and not even take the time to remove all your clothes or pajamas? How often do you have a sex with little or no foreplay or even kissing? How often does sex take less than five minutes from first kiss to final orgasm? Sex becomes a simple release of sexual energy and not the intimate love making it supposed to be. Couples know they are supposed to meet the need for orgasm of their spouse. So they do that. I'm not saying it isn't mutually beneficial. I'm not saying one person has sexual fulfillment, and the other doesn't. I am not saying it is not enjoyable. In my mind, sex is like pizza. All pizza is good, but some is great. We are satisfied with store bought frozen pizza instead of a good Chicago pie. My point is we treat sex as if it is a task to be done instead of an intimate experience with my lover. Just like the rest of your home life, little planning or preparation goes into your sex life. Your entire existence in your marriage and family is simply completing the task for the day or for the week. It's boring.

The point of this book is simple. Your marriage relationship can be, should be, will be your happiest place on the planet. All we have to do is go back to our first love for each other. We need to be best friends. From that point of love and relationship, our sex life will grow and thrive.

BFF

When I say the words, "best friend", what do you think of? If you thought of someone from your childhood, maybe even high school or college, then something is off in your marriage. The word best friend should immediately throw an image of your husband or wife into your mind. If you thought of them, or if you remembered someone else, what makes or made them a best friend?

I grew up with a friend named John Conn. You should read his book about growing up in a poor rural family, "Red Beans and Taters". We met in third grade but were just classmates. In fourth grade, for some reason, we clicked. I walked into homeroom, saw him, and we were instantly great friends. We became inseparable for the next decade. I was the best man in his wedding and he was the one in mine. We spent time together. We laughed and joked. We cried when his mother died. We traveled and did things. We played ball and hung out. We worked together and went to church together. He is the first person I witnessed to after I gave my life to Christ and was one of the first people I led to Jesus. We were best friends because we did life, all of it, together. As much as we were together, we could be together more. We just did life with each other.

That is the key to being a best friend. You are together. You do life together. In high school, either in class or hanging out, there were always other people there with us. The thing is, WE were there with other people. We arrived and left in the same car. We went to parties together. We went to games together. When a lot of people were going to do something, we went there together. It was us and them.

This should describe the surface of your relationship with your husband or wife. I say the surface because a real together connectedness transcends just being best friends. With your spouse, it is US versus the world. We are one. It is not me, my wife and the kids. It is US. WE also have children. I will write about this in a few chapters.

I thought through aspects of what it means to be a BFF. I will give a little taste here and then devote a chapter to the big things which make you the best friend of your spouse. My wife is the most important person in the world to me, and I tell my kids that. The children are a distant second, and the rest of humanity is a distant third. Nothing touches the relationship we have.

So, what are signs or trademarks of a BFF? A BFF enjoys life with you. You know they like being around you. They want to share the fun times of life in your presence. Denise and I spoke at a conference in the States. Some friends of ours attended it and we hung out in their room afterwards. We talked and laughed until tears. It was a great time of funny stories and quick jokes. The next day I told him, "I enjoyed last night. Denise and I laughed several times in our room, thinking of the conversation. Laughter is good medicine." He looked at me and in a moment of vulnerability said, "You know Joe, I do not remember the last time we laughed, seriously laughed. We don't really enjoy life anymore. It felt good." I appreciated his honesty, and we chatted some about it. We enjoy life with our best friend. That is one reason we are such good friends. If I did not enjoy being around someone, I would look for reasons to avoid them. Sadly, this describes many marriages. We look for reasons to avoid being with each other. Our work, errands and children's activities are honestly just excuses to not be with each other. If your spouse is your BFF, you want to be with them. Best friends enjoy each other's company.

Next, a genuine friend accepts you as you are and helps you become better than you are. They don't just accept you. They challenge you. They know all of your strengths and your weaknesses, your good character and the bad. They do this great balancing act. They do not judge or belittle you yet seek to push you to improved living. A best friend is an open door to a stairway up. Inviting and welcoming while lifting you to new heights. They encourage you. When I perform a wedding ceremony, in the typical location of "Do you promise to", I say this.

"Do you promise to commit yourself to a life of helping him/her become who God has created them to be? Do you promise to help them be better?"

That is one role of a best friend. We help the other person become more than they could be without us. In Genesis, God referred to it as a "Helpmeet" or, as some translations put it, "Helper".

Let me interject here and say that today in our culture, that word 'helper' or 'helpmeet' has a negative connotation. Today it seems that being a 'helper' isn't as important as being the one helped. We see it more like an assistant to a more important person. The term 'helpmeet' in years past has been used by chauvinistic men to try and put women down. It was used by men who wanted to elevate themselves and esteem themselves at the cost of women's subjugation. Yes, the Bible uses the term helpmeet for Eve, but it wasn't in the derogatory way that it has been used by those seeking their own agenda. I want to challenge that thinking. The Holy Spirit is named the Helper. Jesus said that it was better for Him, Jesus, to leave the disciples so that He could send The Helper to them. The One who would be able to empower them to take the Gospel and change the world....not an easy task for a rag tag band of nobodies. The Holy Spirt is just as much God the Father and Jesus are. The triune God. They are One. In Genesis when God called Eve, Adam's helpmeet, He was not saying she was an accessory of Adam. She was her own person, as much as the Holy Spirit is a separate person than Jesus or God the Father, yet still One God. Each individual, yet completely unified, another mystery of marriage that I will touch on more later. For now I want us to reprogram our minds from thinking that helping one another, being a helpmeet, makes us less important. Being a helper makes us like the Holy Spirit. Isn't that what we want? To be more like God?

Now back to being your spouse's BFF.

A BFF listens to you. They hear what you say and know what you did not say. They are interested in your story and your stories. They are in tune with your life and want to understand what is happening in and to you. They are emotionally supportive and allow your story to include bad and sad times. Criticism is rare and only given when they believe you can grow from it. You love being with your best friend because you can talk to them. As I write this, my 21-year-old is on the phone with her boyfriend, again. They talk all the time. They are becoming best friends.

A BFF is loyal. They always have your back. You can

depend on them. If you need someone to talk to, loan you a $10, or give you a hand moving the sofa, you call them. Their loyalty goes behind your back as well. They speak well of you to others and refuse to hear evil about you.

They deal with conflict honestly and forgive instantly. There is no such thing as unforgiveness in a best friendship.

They spend large amounts of time together.

They help you become like Jesus.

These are just a few of the things BFF's do.

If you think about it, you used to be best friends with each other. Remember how it worked with you? Before you were married, you had a few good friends, but after dating your husband/wife for a while, they became the most important person to you. The romantic comedies are correct in their stereotype of new couples shutting out all their single friends. We become inseparable. We want to spend all our time with each other. I remember Denise and I would see each other at school, eat school lunch together, chat for 30 minutes in the parking lot after the last bell, and then call on the phone to talk for hours at night. We went out every Friday and Saturday night and then went to church on Sunday mornings and nights. We could not talk enough or be together too much. My children texted their boyfriends/girlfriends so much before marriage, they never seemed to put their phones down. There was no doubt about who they wanted to be with, who they wanted to talk to, and who they wanted to hear from.

Then, one day, after a few years of marriage and maybe a child, you wake up next to your life business partner instead of your best friend. This person beside you helps you and you help them in the logistics of life, but not the joy of it. You no longer spend large amounts of time communicating and talking. Now all you do is short sentences and/or grunts. You don't talk about the future, dreams or plans. You give quick news reports of the day's events and assign tomorrow's activities. Your phone calls went from hours to minutes to a text. Stoic nods replaced the laughter. What happened?

There are many detours that cause us to leave the BFF Highway. One of the most common is unforgiveness. Borrowing from Paul Tripp in his book, "What Did You Expect", I have adapted a definition of a Christian marriage. I share it with couples in premarital counseling. I tell them, "A Christian marriage comprises two forgiven people forgiving each other. The bottom line is others will hurt you. Your spouse will intentionally and unintentionally sin against you. They will disappoint and sadden you. The longer you are together, the more often it will happen. You must learn two things. First, rest in the truth of your forgiveness found in Christ. Second, learn to forgive instantly, completely and without being asked. If you do not forgive them, then the point of your unforgiveness is the exit ramp you took to leave your best friendship. There is no such thing as a best friend you refuse to forgive. There is an ex-best friend you have chosen to not forgive.

A huge issue we have in growing together in our friendship is distraction. There are so many things, good things, that clamor for our attention. It is easy to get distracted. We jokingly quote the movie "Up" as a reminder. We will emphatically say, "Squirrel!" to point out something has stolen our attention. On multiple occasions, I have counseled married people to eliminate electronics from their home. Denise and I got rid of our television in 1993. Our oldest son was four. We talked about it and Denise said, "You know, taking a nap is more beneficial than television. Why watch shows and movies about families doing things together when we could actually do things together? Forget moral issues. It is poor time management." Our children grew up without a TV in the home. I am 59 years old and I have never played a game of golf. It takes too much time away from what is truly important, my family. I do not own a single computer game and have never had one installed on my system. Computer games are typically solo events, and I am not alone. I have a wife. A BBF. We get distracted by entertainment, sports, games, stress, finances, children and careers. We have conquered the marriage aspect of life and now move on to new conquests. If you want to expand in your friendship with each other, you must shrink in the things which stop or slow your growth. I call it weeding the garden. Remove the things which take away time and energy you could devote to growing fruit in your relationships.

We also refocus on other things. This differs from distraction. Distractions are unintentional and sometimes unknowing. A refocus means you put something in front of your relationship with each other. The two biggest things we refocus on are the blessings of children and careers. I remember, over 34 years ago, when it was just the two of us. It was so easy to stay focused on Denise and to invest in her. We had one another and focused on that relationship ahead of everything else.

In 1989, my son was born, and I went from being a husband to also being a dad. Ten more kids followed. I now have eleven children and eight grandchildren. Denise and I have been very intentional in refusing to become child-centered or child-first. We seek to give our relationship as husband and wife greater priority than dad and mom. It is difficult. The children need me. They crave my attention and love. I love them in a way that only a parent can fathom. There is this deep God-given bond. Therefore, many people quickly go from being a husband with a child and turn into a father with a wife. We focus our energy on our children and parenting. Wives who are also moms are tempted to do the same.

We also do this with our careers. This was my experience I shared earlier. I focused on the success of my church and ignored the growth of my marriage. Our motivations are pure. In my case, I wanted to succeed at church and bring people to Jesus. My wife told me, "I cannot, and should not, compete with the gospel and plight of the lost. But I feel like I have to in order to get any attention from you." That is because I was focused on my church. She felt like she was in a competition with my career, and she was loosing. Loosing my attention, my focus, and my passion. Those were being poured into my career. This can be especially difficult if one of your careers is one that is considered 'noble' like ministry, or caring for the sick and injured, or caring for/teaching children, or sacrificially helping others as fire-fighters or law enforcement. It's extremely difficult for a spouse to feel like they must compete with that kind of career without appearing selfish, so don't put them in that position. Demonstrate actively to them that they are first.

We want to succeed in the workplace in order to provide

for our families. We want our children and ourselves to have a better life than we did. Of course, we always define better in financial and material terms, yet better is what we want, and that takes our focus from our family itself.

Another reason we refocus on our careers, is we receive recognition and appreciation there. The kids don't care if you worked extra hard to be a good wife and mom. They take you for granted. You do not get awards, promotions or pay raises. You get ignored and taken for granted by spouse and children. Your spouse and children might not appreciate the extra hours your put in for your career, they might even resent it even though you are doing it for their betterment. When the people at work notice and appreciate the sacrifices you make, this causes us to pour more energy into our career than our relationship with our husband or wife.

Distraction or a refocus causes us to stop devoting time to the growth and cultivation of our marriage relationship. Our friendship is no longer a priority. Friendship is a crop that takes work to grow fruit. It must be tended, weeded, nurtured, and cultivated. If we are not intentional in growing our friendship, then by accident, it will atrophy and shrink. We must put effort into focusing on, improving, and developing our friendship or we will coast to a stop.

Many times, other friends enter and take the title of BFF. When we choose to not forgive our spouse, when we get distracted by other things, when we loose our focus, and we no longer work on growing in our friendship, we inadvertently replace our spouse with someone or something else. Like the movie tag line, "There can be only one." By definition the best is singular. I can have lots of friends and I can have lots of good friends, but I can only have one BEST friend. If we spend time quantity and quality time with other people or activities other than our spouse, that person or activity can take that place of our spouse who is to meant to be the best friend in our lives.

Do not forget both sin and Satan. Personal sin in our hearts and lives will destroy our relationship with each other. Sin is never an individual activity. It always spills over onto those closest to us. A great example is pornography. I have talked to probably a hundred men over the decades engaged in the sin of pornography. Their sinful lusts destroyed their relationship with their wives. Every one of them thought it was a personal and victimless sin. That is not the case. It mars your perception of sex, love and women. It distorts expectations and causes frustration in your real life. It is perversion and will pervert your worldview and poison your marriage. Sin destroys. If you, men or women, are involved in pornography I urge you right now, before you even finish this book to find a Godly man if you are a man or a Godly woman if you are a woman to walk with you on the path of repentance, accountability, and restoration from the sin of pornography.

Satan is real and wants to kill, steal, and destroy your marriage. He exists. He is alive. He is a threat. He is our enemy. He is the father of lies and a murderer. He desires your pain. He will do what he can to destroy your marriage by any means possible. If we are not on guard for his lies and deception, we have probably already believed some of them.

BFF Reflection Questions

1. Tell each other about your best friends in each stage of life such as elementary school, high school, and after graduation. Share a fun memory. What was it that made 'this' friend your 'best' one?

2. Do you enjoy being around each other? Why or why not? What makes your relationship enjoyable, or what is stopping it from being enjoyable?

3. How much do you talk? How active do you listen? What do you talk about? What do you not talk about?

4. Is there anything you haven't forgiven in your relationship? Your friendship will stop growing at the detour of unforgiveness.

5. Has something or someone, even children, distracted you from pursuing friendship with your husband or wife? What can you do about it?

6. Are you focusing and/or prioritizing other areas of life more than your marriage friendship? What is your focus and how can you re-focus on each other?

7. In Joe's opinion, one of the greatest detriments to strengthening our marriage are children. Instead of being a husband who has children, we become fathers who have a wife. The same thing happens to women. Are your children more important to you than your spouse? Why? If you have fallen into

being child-centered, how can you begin to change that?

Learning To Love

The first book I wrote is on discipleship. It is called "Discipleship of the Heart." You should buy it on kindle or paperback. It is good. I know it is because the author told me. I have a few chapters on love in it. As I am writing this chapter on love, I realized. I could just borrow heavily from the material already published. After all, I am the author, so I don't need to worry about plagiarism. I tell you this because if you already have "Discipleship of the Heart" you will recognize much of it is in this chapter. If not, when you read it, you will recognize this chapter is in it. ;) I equate it to preaching the same sermon to different churches. I have a great message, so why limit it to one group? So, here you go.

When I was in high school, I had friends who were in track. I tried to be. I was even on the track team when I was a freshman. I ran the 880. I have what may be a record in the State of Texas. I came in last (not second to last, not near the back--LAST) in every single race. I tell my kids that even before I knew Christ; I took part in a ministry of making people feel better about themselves. I was the person who made second-to-last possible. I totally stunk at track. I was also pretty bad at baseball, not good at basketball, third string in football and mediocre in tennis. As I evaluate my high school sports record, I ask myself why I was in sports. I figured this out my senior year and played nothing. I marvel it took me that long to admit I was pathetic. However, I was in sports and that allowed me to have friends in sports. One of my friends in track was good at the high jump and at pole vaulting. Occasionally a few of us would get together and just practice jumping. It was straightforward. You had three tries to clear the bar. If you cleared it, then you raised it another inch. This kept going until you could no longer clear the bar. Your goal was to keep raising the bar. It was a noble goal for me, because I cannot jump over a sheet of notebook paper.

There is something in the Bible that will make you feel you are me looking up at an 18' pole vault bar with the challenge of clearing it without a pole. A truth that is simply beyond our ability, yet it is our responsibility.

God's love for His children is unconditional. It has NO CONDITIONS. Therefore, nothing can separate us from the love of God. It is freely and completely given to us by Him with no condition at all being put upon it or us. If it had only one condition...even a tiny one, then it would not be unconditional and it would be possible to be separated from it.

Let me explain it in a way that I have used in marriage counseling and in premarital counseling. I first used this when a couple came to me because the wife had committed adultery. The wife had come to the husband and confessed the sexual sin after being convicted by the Holy Spirit and repenting of it. She wasn't 'caught' in the act. She sincerely regretted her sin, confessed, and repented.

The husband wanted a divorce. As I talked to them, it soon became obvious (as it always does) that the adultery was just a huge sin (you understand what I mean by this) in a history of sins linked together. It also became clear (as it almost always does) that the husband had failed his wife in many areas. He had not committed adultery, but neither had he loved her as Christ loved the church. I explained God's love to them. I pointed out how God loved the husband. I took him to Bible passages that revealed God's love for him during his own sin, and in spite of it. I had him confess that he believed God had loved him in eternity past and would continue to love Him without even the tiniest condition throughout all time.

He believed this and was thankful for it. Let me take you into my office that day.

"So, you see God loves you? That He loves you in Christ, and that His love for you is unconditional?" I asked him.

"Yes."

I continued, "If you were to sin, would God love you less than He does right now? Or if you were to do some super Christian thing like go to the mission field, would it make God love you more than this moment?"

"No. God loves me unconditionally. But what does this have to do with us?" He wanted to know.

"Let's look at a passage of Scripture together. Ephesians 5 says this: 'Husbands, love your wives as Christ loved the church.' 1 Peter tells us we are to love our wives 'in the same way' that Jesus loves us. He could see where I was going with this principle, but the illustration that I used rocked his world. It was so powerful that I have used it several times in marriage conferences to illustrate God's unconditional love.

"If you love your wife unconditionally like Jesus loves you, that means that you will love her just as much when she is in bed with another man as you do when she is having sex with you. Your love is not conditioned on who she has sex with."

Our conversation continued.

"I will not love my wife if she has sex with another man." He insisted.

"Okay. I can see your point. You will love your wife on one condition. She must agree to never have sex with him again."

"Yes."

"So, she agrees to never have sex with him, but she really wants to have sex with him. Is that okay?"

"No! She cannot want to have sex with him! She must not even see him."

"Okay, let's write this down. You have three conditions that I think anyone would agree with. She cannot have sex with him. She cannot want to have sex with him. She cannot see him."

"So, she just emails him, privately messages him, and talks to him on the phone. Is that good enough for you?" He expanded his list to include the prohibition of these items and we summarized it up by a total lack of contact of any kind...the list grew. It also incorporated emotions and desires.

"Now, our list is at about 10 items. Not that big of a deal. But I just thought of something. What if it isn't this guy, but another co-worker that she wants to have sex with?" The list now included all co-workers and all lustful thinking. It included all non-work contact with any other man. It grew to cover her internet browsing and her movie and television choices. By now, he saw that his one condition was not one condition.

"Here is the thing." I said, "There are only two types of love. We either love like God does: unconditionally; or we love like people do and put conditions on our love. What does God want us to do?"

What he realized that day, and what I think we all soon realize for ourselves, is that unconditional love is a great thing to receive, but when it comes to giving it, the bar is pretty high. Jesus even referred to this in Luke 6 by saying that people of the kingdom of God are to love others who don't love us, who abuse and misuse us, and who hurt us. If we only love the ones who love us, how is that any different than sinners (those who are not of the kingdom of God)? Anyone can love someone who loves you back. That's fairly easy.

I am talking about raising the bar. Let's see how high God has actually raised it.

The Father loves us. How does He love us? What is the type of love He has for us?

Just as the Father has loved Me, I have also loved you; abide in My love. (John 15:9)

I in them and You in Me, that they may be perfected in unity, so that the world may know that You sent Me, and loved them, even as You have loved Me. (John 17:23)

and I have made Your name known to them, and will make it known, so that the love with which You loved Me may be in them, and I in them." (John 17:26)

Imagine if you can, and we can't, but try to imagine how the Father loves the Son. Picture the passion, the emotion, the unbroken direction of His heart. God the Father loves

God the Son with pure, perfect love.

Now, let your imagination go even farther than this. God the Father says that He loves YOU the same way, in the same manner, and with the same love that He has for the Son! The Father loves us like He loves Jesus. It is not just in the same way, but with the SAME LOVE. God loves His children with the same love that He loves His Son! Wow! It gets even more profound.

A new commandment I give to you, that you love one another, even as I have loved you, that you also love one another. (John 13:34)

This is My commandment, that you love one another, just as I have loved you. (John 15:12)

Therefore be imitators of God, as beloved children; and walk in love, just as Christ also loved you and gave Himself up for us, an offering and a sacrifice to God as a fragrant aroma. (Ephesians 5:1-2)

Husbands, love your wives, just as Christ also loved the church and gave Himself up for her (Ephesians 5:25)

Do not let this pass you by. Follow the line of thought and raise your bar.

God the Father loves me 'just as' and with the 'same love' that He loves the Son.

Jesus Christ the Son loves me with the 'same love' and 'just as' the Father loves Him.

I am then told that I am to love other people 'just as' Jesus loves me.

I am to love other people the way that Jesus loves me.

Jesus loves me the way the Father loves Him.

Therefore, I am to love other people the way that the Father loves the Son!

This is why the world will know we are His disciples by our love. It is because our love is the love of God! It is heavenly, unconditional love. It is love not based on the worth, the merit, or the actions of the one receiving it. It is the love of the Father.

Imagine your marriage with this one principle in place. You love your husband/wife with the same love and in the same way Jesus loves you. What would happen in your home and heart if you gave and received unconditional love to each other?

The bar is high. Let's be honest. It is too high for us to clear. It is like me in high school track. We cannot and will not do this. We are incapable. So, what do we do?

My wife loves Starbucks Frappuccino's. Since we lived in Bolivia, she rarely could get them. One time, I was in our local grocery store, and they had them for sale. It was a month before Christmas, so I bought them all. I paid $3 a bottle for 143 bottles. I had to go to an ATM and get the money. It was the best Christmas present I have ever given to my wife. For the next several months, every morning she would wake up and one of our kids would bring her a cold Frappuccino. My four-year-old daughter took one to her in the morning, and with all the pride of a young child helping mom said, "Mommy, I brought you a Crap-u-chino". She enunciated each part of her new word particularly focused on the first syllable. It was over 10 years ago, and to this day we call them Crap-u-chinos. We renamed the product.

This happened to love. It is a little different, because we have not only renamed but have also replaced the genuine thing. We have misunderstood what it means to love for so long we now believe our distortion of the truth is the truth. For example, if you look up a definition of the word, "love", in a dictionary you will find it wrapped in emotional or sexual terms. Love, it seems, is a pleasant feeling or good sex. Neither one of those are unconditional actions. Therefore, we don't understand how to love. We have redefined the term.

There is no doubt God desires for husbands and wives to love each other. It is our love for each other, our unconditional love, which makes marriage unique.

God expands this teaching on in the famous chapter on love, 1 Corinthians 13. In the first view verses we learn loving others is such a chief priority that if we do not have love, nothing else we do matters.

If I speak with the tongues of men and of angels, but do not have love, I have become a noisy gong or a clanging cymbal. If I have the gift of prophecy, and know all mysteries and all knowledge; and if I have all faith, so as to remove mountains, but do not have love, I am nothing. And if I give all my possessions to feed the poor, and if I surrender my body to be burned, but do not have love, it profits me nothing. (1 Corinthians 13:1-3)

Without love, all we say is a loud noise. Without love,

we waste all of our spiritual gifts. Without love, all of our knowledge is ignorance. Without love, all of our faith and all of our sacrifices are worthless. Without love I do nothing, accomplish nothing, and am nothing. Love is not merely an emotion, it is the foundation of all other virtues and actions.

Love is not an emotion, it is an active force in our lives. It changes me.

Love is patient, love is kind and is not jealous; love does not brag and is not arrogant, does not act unbecomingly; it does not seek its own, is not provoked, does not take into account a wrong suffered, does not rejoice in unrighteousness, but rejoices with the truth; bears all things, believes all things, hopes all things, endures all things. (1 Corinthians 13:4-7)

Look at 1 Corinthians 13:4-7. In the early part of my Christian journey, and my ministry, I always viewed this as a "to-do list". I taught love is not something you feel, it is something you do. I loved to quote the platitude which said, "Love is a verb not a noun." I preached a series called "How To Be A Better Lover" based on this passage. My series was full of things to do. Love is patient. I therefore preached a four-point sermon on how to be patient. Love is kind. No worries, I have three steps to kindness. I did this throughout these verses. I had an entire sermon on each "love is" declaration. It was a great series. I loved it, and so did my church. I only wish it had been the teaching of the Bible.

This is not a "to-do list". It is a checklist. It is a list to evaluate myself by. How am I measuring up? I am called to love others unconditionally. How do I know if I am loving this way? If I am, then I will be kind and forgiving. See the difference? If this is a to-do list, then being kind produces love. If this is a checklist, then being kind shows that I love, and transversely unkindness reveals a lack of love. The first idea is patience causes love. The second is it is the effect of love. This understanding makes all the difference in the world. This checklist is a way for us to gauge our own walk with Christ. I need Jesus. I need the gospel. I can see that when I test my love life by this checklist. I don't need love that is a product of my effort. This is the exact opposite of the gospel message. It is not effort. It is grace. I need grace-love.

This is where we redefine the terms and leave our Crap-u-chino love for the genuine thing. What I am about to explain in my next two points is life changing. I know because it changed my life. This is something pastors say a lot, and most of the time it is hyperbole or an outright exaggeration. Here, it is truth.

Love is a verb. Love is something you do. Love is action. That is what 1 Corinthians 13:1-7 teach us. Love influences and changes. Love produces action. However, the phrase I used to 'love' to say, "Love is a verb, not a noun" is not completely true. Love is a verb. It is also a noun.

Love is not only something I do, it is something I receive.

Love is a product. I am the receiving agent of a product

called love.

Beloved, let us love one another, for love is from God;
and everyone who loves is born of God and knows God. (1
John 4:7)

In the first part of this verse, we see love is action. We
are to love one another. However, there is a key part of this
verse that is often overlooked. Love is from God. The love
in our lives that influences and changes us and allows us to
love others in a way that shows know God is something
from God. It is something He gives us.

But the fruit of the Spirit is love, joy, peace, patience,
kindness, goodness, faithfulness (Galatians 5:22)

This famous passage contrasts the works of the flesh
with the fruit of the Spirit. The fruits of the Spirit are
something we receive from God. As we abide in the Holy
Spirit, and He fills us, God gives us spiritual fruit. One of
those fruits is love. Just as an additional push towards
understanding love does come from God, look at a couple
of those other fruits and you see 1 Corinthians lists them
where God describes love. Love is a product of the Holy
Spirit. It is something the Holy Spirit gives us.

When I am teaching on this aspect, I like to use a
tangible illustration. I will ask someone in the audience to
bring me something. It might be a chair, or a lectern, or
something there near the stage and in sight. When they
bring it, I ask them everything about it. How was it made?
What type of materials did they use? How long did it take

them to make it? I ask question after question about the manufacturing process until their inability to answer frustrates them. I point out all of my questions were moot. It was not their task to manufacture the product. All they needed to do was deliver the product.

When we are in the States, we take full advantage of Amazon and other mailing services. We buy a myriad of products online. After we buy something, they deliver it to our home. For example, I purchased a new laptop. I eagerly waited for it. One day about a week later, a brown truck pulled into my driveway. Do you know what the driver did? Do you think he pulled into my driveway and opened up a box of tools and supplies? Imagine him with a circuit board and a soldering iron dutifully connecting the various parts of the laptop in his truck. He finishes manufacturing of my laptop and hands it to me before driving to the next home and building a diffuser for essential oils in their driveway and starts to assemble the lawnmower for his last stop.

That is not what happens. The driver is not the manufacturer. It is not his job to create or make anything. His job is simple. He is to deliver a product. The box has an address on it. He takes the box to the address and gives it to the person on the label. My daughter Hope worked for FedEx. One of her jobs was to solve issues with undeliverable items. She researched and tried to find the correct address where the delivery driver could take the package. At no point did she, the driver, or anyone with FedEx work on what is in the package. Their job is not to assemble, it is to deliver.

For too long we have confused our role. We look at love as something we manufacture. We have even changed the name of sex and call it "lovemaking". We look at all the people in our lives and try to manufacture the love they need.

Here is the crux of the issue. God has commanded us to love others unconditionally with His love. We try to love others unconditionally with our love. The love of Joe is not unconditional. So, since I cannot love unconditionally with my love, I give up trying and I love others with a cheap religious imitation which always results in some conditions being placed upon it. It is not the love of Joe others need. That love I can do. Joe's love is religiously, morally, ethnically, selfishly and socio-economically based. My love is so pathetic.

God commanded us to love others with His love. I do not manufacture His love. God did not give us the ability to make His love. Stay with me on this. I cannot make God's love, but I can possess it. I can receive it and I can give it. I cannot make it. I am human. I am not God.

So, how can I love others with God's love if I cannot manufacture God's love? I do so by receiving it from Him. It is a fruit of the Holy Spirit. God wants to love my wife. He gives me His love and tells me to deliver it to the other person. I am not called to manufacture His love, no more than the UPS driver builds a computer in my driveway. I am called to deliver His love. God has His love with the address of my wife written on the label. I am to pick up His love from Him and deliver it to my wife. In the same way UPS delivers a package to your doorstep, you are to deliver God's love to other people. You receive it from God. You take it to others. I don't have to try to pretend my love is unconditional because it is not. However, I can receive

God's unconditional love and take it to others.

As I abide in the Spirit and walk in Him, He produces and gives me His fruit. One of the fruits He produces is love. He also gives me kindness and patience among other virtues. As I evaluate how I treat my wife, if I do not see the fruit of love being manifested in my life (the checklist), then I can know at this moment I am not abiding in Christ. If I were abiding in Him, I would bear much fruit. My lack of fruit is the proof I am not abiding. The checklist revealed the sin of my heart. God's love for my wife did not vacillate. It was steadfast. My love changed, and the change revealed my need for Christ. Love is a noun. Love is not just something I do; it is something I receive.

One more vital thing to understand about love.

Love is not just something I do; it is something I receive.
Love is not just something I receive; it is Someone I am with. Love is a Person.

My favorite movie series of all time is the Star Wars world. I remember watching the first one, Episode IV, over ten times when I was in High School. I saw every one of them, to this present day and the spinoff and backstory movies, on opening day. It is a family tradition to be there. My daughters have even had their photos taken on the red carpet with the real R2D2! We love Star Wars. One thing we must avoid, however, is allowing movie theology to affect our own worldview. This has happened in a small way with love. Christians view love as a 'force'. I even own a collection of songs and the title of the cd is "The Power Of Love". We think love is this impersonal attribute or virtue which causes change. This is not true.

Love is a Person.

The one who does not love does not know God, for God is love. (1 John 4:8)

We have come to know and have believed the love which God has for us. God is love, and the one who abides in love abides in God, and God abides in him. (1 John 4:16)

Two times God makes a powerful statement. He says, "God is love."

One thing we will see over and over in this book on discipleship is this: It is all about God. Over and over, we will come back to the heart of the gospel. God wants to have a love relationship with me, and He has done everything possible to do so. He loves me. My life is complete in Him. Not in doing what He says, but in HIM. Love is the same thing. He is the focus.

Let me put the lesson together for you.

God is love. I am to focus on Him. I confess my sins and make sure my heart is pure as I abide, live and walk in Him. As I am with Him, I understand and see things from His perspective. I realize the importance of love and His call for me to love others with His love.

While I am abiding in Him and becoming more like Him through the ministry of the Holy Spirit, I receive the fruits of the Spirit in my life. The Holy Spirit gives me the fruit of love. The fruit of the Holy Spirit works in my life and I have His love, patience, kindness, etc. I am changed by His love.

I, through Him, understand His love is not only for me. I am to be a conduit of His love and give His love to others. I can deliver the unconditional love of God to the people in my life. It is no longer the love of Joe. It is His Presence, His Spirit, and His Love in me. I can love others unconditionally because I am not doing it. He is doing it in me and through me.

One day when I pastored in the States, I came home from the office and to be honest I had experienced a very trying day. In the ministry there are some days where people are not nice to their pastor. There are days that just push those of us who are in full-time ministry to the limits. This was one of those days. When I pulled into my driveway, the trashcans were still at the road and one was knocked over. The kids know they are supposed to get the cans at lunch and put them back in the garage. As I pulled up, I had to stop and get a bicycle out of the way so I could pull into the garage itself. I walked into the house, and I was ready to transfer my nasty day to other people. I said something, I cannot remember what, to my wife in a snippy manner. She answered me and a few moments later I was rude again. The third time she turned to me and I was hoping to get the response I had been pushing for. Instead, she looked into my eyes and said, "Babe, I can see you have had a bad day. You seem upset." She walked over and took me into an enormous hug. After about 30 seconds of silently hugging me, she said, "Is there anything I can do, any way I can serve you?" She destroyed my desire to be mean. Her fruit of patience, kindness, peace, gentleness and love overcame me.

When she tells her viewpoint, it includes her running to the cross six or seven times and asking Jesus to fill her with the Spirit so she could respond in a manner which would glorify Him and help me. She says she had to check her heart and have the Holy Spirit stop her words several times. She prayed for me. Her focus was not on the injustice of the moment and how I was treating her. She was looking at Jesus and what He wanted to do at the moment. This is a great example of what I am referring to. I was not in the kitchen with Denise. I was in the kitchen with God and Denise. He was fully present, and she knew it. His Person gave her through the Spirit the ability to perceive what was going on through His eyes and also His fruit. She then delivered His fruit to me.

We can live this scenario out in every relationship we have. We should live it out. This is how the world knows we are His disciples, by our love.

Best friends love each other. If we love our spouse with the unconditional, Spirit-filled fruit of God it transforms us.

Love Reflection Questions

1. Do you feel as if your spouse loves you
    unconditionally? Do you love him/her without
    conditions?

2. Talk about how deep God's love is for us. Jesus said
    we should love each other the way He loves us. He
    said He loves us the same way the Father loves Him.
    So we should love each other the same way the
    Father loves Jesus! How would this flesh out in your
    home?

3. If you look at 1 Corinthians 13 as a checklist of your
    love, how do you measure up? Does God describe
    your marriage in this chapter? What needs to
    change?

4. Love is a fruit. Love is not just something we do, it is
    something we receive. Do you maintain a constant
    relationship with the Holy Spirit? Are you filled
    with, led by and walking in the Spirit? Do you see,
    better yet, do others see the fruits of the Holy Spirit
    flowing from your life?

5. Love is not just something we do, it is something we
    receive. Love is not just something we receive, it is
    Someone we are with. God is Love. If we abide in
    God we abide in Love. How is your on-going
    relationship with the Father? Your marriage
    relationship will never be greater or deeper than your
    relationship with God since it is that relationship

which enables the other. Is God real in your life, or are you simply going through the motions?

Best Fellowship Forever

I do a lot. It is hard-wired into me. I evangelize the lost, pastor a church, manage a missionary guesthouse, work with orphans and children, run a construction ministry, help business as mission projects, host evangelistic crusades, organize medical missions, work with clean water ministry, teach conferences and do one-on-one discipleship. God built me to move. One of the hardest things for me to do is slow down. God created me to move. I have always been high octane. This character strength has probably been one of my greatest relational weaknesses. There are other people like this. I often find my to-do list to be so demanding I forget my I-do person. I told her "I Do." I promised to love her with all I am and all I can be. That was before eleven children, ministry and missions, pastoring and discipling, living on another continent, working with the poor and hurting, etc. Now, I just don't have time to devote to her. There are things I have to do. I take our relationship for granted and think that because we were once close, we still are best friends. I am not alone. I have to stop with getting projects done and focus on us.

Best friends love to be together. We called it 'hang out' when I was in high school. We would just hang out. No purpose other than being somewhere with each other. Couples start dating and a large part of their time together is hanging out. They want to be together. Throughout the dating and early part of our marriage, we want to hang out. We love to be together.

When did it become a problem in our lives? Why is it that being together, especially alone and together, interferes with what we think is getting life done? Isn't he/she your life? What is more important than this relationship? Honestly? Look at your life and the answer to that question is probably everything. It is so easy to allow everything and anything to take priority over your marriage growth. I know that by looking at what you spend your time doing and what you think about. I know that because it happened to me. I allowed my calling and career to be my priority.

It is another of the cyclical aspects of life. Best friends spend time together. When you spend time with someone, you become closer to them. I hang out with my friend and the friendship deepens because we hang out together. The opposite is true as well. If you do not invest time in a relationship, you will get the return on your investment, which is nothing. If you are not being proactive and intentional in your marriage relationship, then it is not growing. If you are not spending time with your spouse, not in their presence, but with them, they are not your best friend.

Denise often reminds me of this. She will say, "You are here, but not here. Where are you?" She will gently ask me what I am doing on my device. I believe most couples spend more time on social media and electronic games than they invest in actually being with each other. For a while we enforced a "no electronics" policy for our bedroom. I really had to learn how to deal with this, since my office was at home. One day we ate dinner. We ate around 5:00. I then said, "I am going to finish a couple of things." I went to the office to return an email and work on a budget spreadsheet for the church. My quick trip to the office ended at a little before 9:00 pm. I apologized and told her the time "flew by".

Denise and I talked about it in our room later because I knew I hurt her. She asked me, "When was the last time three hours flew by because you were with me?" It was a brilliant question and called me to reevaluate priorities. If she is my best friend, why do I ignore her and spend so much time on my device? Why do I behave as if an iPhone is my friend and my wife is a task? Why is it our spouses interfere with our plans but our plans never interfere with our spouses?

Best friends love to be together. Period. You want to be with, to hang out with, your best friend. At some point shortly after marriage, without a doubt after children, our purpose changed from being with each other to getting things done with or without the other.

Rescript your purpose. We are always so busy with our tasks we do not have time for each other. So, we divide and conquer. One spouse goes to the store and the other spouse gets other things done. If we go to the store together, we make a map for the most efficient team shopping. This just happened and reveals how difficult it is for me to apply this truth to my own life. Denise and I went to the store.

I said, "Let's split the list. I will go grab the detergent and foil while you get the meat. Then I will get these two items and you grab those. Meet you at the checkout."

"Wait." Denise said. "Why are you in such a hurry? What do you do that is so important we can't walk through a store together? If we do your divide and conquer, it will probably save us three minutes. What is so urgent you can't spend three minutes chatting with me in the store?"

Nothing. I just always feel this self-imposed pressure to get this done so I can do that. We get it done because we have other things to do. We want to leave this place because we have other places to go. We are always thinking of something else, somewhere else, with someone else. Whenever we go somewhere, we can't stay long because we have somewhere to go. I bet you even multi-task in bed. We do things on our devices, answer messages, make lists and plan the next day while streaming a show on the computer.

We are too busy for each other.

Stop it.

Don't let life pull you apart. Be together as much as possible. The Bible says we are to be one flesh. We have been joined. One purpose of marriage is to complete each other. We are to be unified.

It is hard to be one if you are always wanting to be in two separate places.

It is hard to be one if you are always doing two separate things.

It is hard to be one if you are never together.

We are to be with each other and help each other. Denise and I re-scripted our view of life. Our focus now is on each other, and what we do is to enable our friendship and fellowship. My wife and I are both followers of Jesus Christ. This means God has called us to intense brotherhood and fellowship. Every aspect of Christian fellowship, every deep and profound part of brotherly love, should be multiplied in a Christian marriage.

The phrase "one another" occurs around 100 times in the New Testament and 59 of those are specific commands teaching us how to and how not to relate to each other. If you have followed Christ for any period of time, you probably know some of these verses. Pastors love to promote small groups with them. Church leaders challenge members to be 'one-another Christians'. I do. I preached through the 'one-anothers' in two of the churches I pastored. I called one of my sermon series, "Camp Weneo". WENeedEachOther.

I also use these a lot in marriage counseling, since the closest 'one another' in our life shares our bed. You are literally one-flesh. Sex is the ultimate one-another as your bodies actually form together into one unit. You do not get more 'one-another' than that. These verses are not for church on Sunday morning. They are not limited to your weekly small group. God gave them to us to teach us how to live.

I am writing a book for Christian families called, "That Verse Applies". The point of the book is the point of the Bible. The verses are to be applied here and now. Rather than being studied, they are to be lived. These verses teach husbands how to live with their wives and vice/versa. They reveal good parenting techniques to us as we treat our children as 'one-another' brothers and sisters in Christ. Do not limit them to people in your small group fellowship. These are imperatives. This means they are commands not suggestions. They do not tell us the best way to live. They teach us how to live. They describe what your home life ought to be. These verses are God's written will for our marriage.

Look at this list and imagine what would happen if this described your marriage relationship. This is the heart of fellowship. I like to say, "Married couples are not just best friends forever, or BFF's. They are to experience the Best Fellowship Forever.

We are BFF squared. We are the most BFF we can be! In the next few pages I will address a few of these one another imperatives. Study them together and seek to apply them, both the ones I mention and the ones I do not. Your marriage is a real fellowship of the ring if you pardon a geek joke. Many of these imperatives bleed into each other. They are nuances of the same overall character trait. Sometimes it is merely a shift of focus. However, God wrote them down individually for us to apply to our lives.

Love one another (John 13:34 - This command occurs at least 16 times).

I covered this in the previous chapter. We are to love each other with God's unconditional love. I believe there are two words which sum up both Christianity and a Christian marriage. Love and forgiveness are those two words. God loves us so much He forgives us in Christ. The forgiveness we have in Christ allows us to experience the love God has for us. We are to love each other. This sounds so simplistic, yet I have spent over thirty years counseling couples who stopped loving each other. They live together, or put up with each other, but they do not pursue love in their marriage. They no longer make love in bed because they do not have love out of bed. They are with each other doing tasks out of bed. The same mindset applies to sex. Let's just get it done. God teaches we are to love each other with a love so incredible it preaches Christ to those who see it. We do not fall out of love. We sinfully stop loving. God does not make loving your husband or wife an option for you to consider. It is a command. You are to love one another with the unconditional love of God.

Forgive one another (Ephesians 4:2, 32; Colossians 3:13).

I will devote a chapter to this topic. In the same manner, we receive God's love and pass it to others. We receive God's forgiveness and mercy and share it with others. This is another one which seems obvious to Christian couples, yet does not happen. We allow anger and bitterness to destroy our families. We are to forgive one another. At the moment, right now, always.

Be devoted to one another (Romans 12:10).

This means we are to focus our attention on the other person. The word devoted can be used as an adjective. It describes someone who commits to a cause. "He is a devoted football fan." If we hear someone described by the adjective, we know they love the object of the description. The word is used to communicate a singular focus. Magazines are devoted to a subject such as hunting or fishing. Sports Illustrated is devoted to the topic of sports. People can be devoted to politics. Whenever you hear someone described by this word, you know the person's passion.

I ask couples this question. "If someone described you to a stranger, would they say, 'He is a devoted husband?' Would they say 'She is devoted to her marriage?' Do people think of the word 'devote' to describe your relationship with each other?"

I am an avid reader of leadership and self-development books. So often they speak to "finding your passion". For a Christian who is married, you have found your passion. It is your spouse. Now, pursue your passion. Be devoted, focused, attentive to each other. Your spouse ought to have a fan club and you are the President, Vice President and number one fan in it. You are the head cheerleader for their team.

My children think I am the greatest thing since sliced bread. They truly respect me. They honor me. They want to be like me. My adult sons seek to imitate my character and my adult daughters want to marry a man like me. This is not because of me. It is because their mom brainwashed them. They grew up watching and hearing the woman they respect most in the world focus on me. She constantly told them I was incredible. She wanted my boys to be like me. She told the girls to look for a man like me. Over and over, she constantly spoke my praise. It indoctrinated the children. I must be something if she is that passionate about me.

How can you be devoted to one-another? First, you must whole-heartedly and without reservations, love your spouse. The whole command is to be devoted to one another in love. I always bring it back to this. Do you love him/her? I do not mean this in a theological affirmation. Do you love him/her? If you emotionally love something, really love it, then you devote yourself to the pursuit of it. If someone tells me they are devoted to Christ yet rarely attend church, never evangelize, do not have personal times of prayer and reading God's Word, are not part of a small group, never give to world missions, and constantly criticize the body of Christ, then I would question their devotion. You are not devoted to Him if you ignore Him and what He loves.

This is true for your spouse. Devotion is an act of love, and love is an act of devotion. Devotion is a conscious decision to love.

Devotion is also a singular focus. It is a way to describe someone's priority. "He is a devoted _____." This tells me one of his priorities. I know he puts this particular thing in front of most other things. I know this is extremely important to him and a large part of his life. In my personal example and story of allowing other things to become my priority, Denise questioned my love for her. My priorities revealed my love and/or lack of it. How could I say I was devoted to her if she wasn't my priority?

Denise does not enjoy sports. She is a self-described "P.E. Hater". She said from early elementary to graduation, she hated going to P.E. She never played organized sports. She doesn't watch sports on television unless it is a family event where we all watch the World Cup Final or some other championship game. She is from Texas so of course she enjoys American football, but doesn't go out of her way to keep up with it.

She married me. I loved sports. I was not good, but I enjoyed them. She pulled up her big girl pants and picked up a racquet so she could learn to play racquetball with me. She is devoted to me and therefore chose to do what I wanted to do as an act of devotion. I think that is a good way to describe it. Devotion is not compartmentalized. I am not devoted to this aspect of my wife but not to that one. We need to be singularly focused holistically on our spouses. Their interests, desires, needs, and dreams become ours. In Texas, there is a proverb. It states, "Love me, love my dog."

The idea is we are a package deal. If you love me, you love mine. You love what I love. Devotion to one-another implies the other person takes priority over the rest of your life. They are not a part of your life. They are one of the reasons you are alive. Devote yourself to one-another. Be passionate about who the other person is and what they want. Devotion is a commitment to concentrate on the other person.

Honor one another above yourselves (Romans 12:10).

The word honor is an idea of respecting someone by elevating them. When you watch a period piece at the movies or on television, the King and Queen sit on an elevated platform. We experience this on a normal basis since we moved to Tamale, Ghana. In Ghana, when we go to visit a village, it is customary to first greet the chief. We wait in the yard outside until called into their hut. The chief sits on animal skins and is slightly elevated above the others in the hut as a way to show honor to him. We seek to show honor so we bow or kneel and then, when given permission, sit on the dirt in front of them. It is a sign of respect to lift them up. For them to be elevated above us shows their importance.

This is how we should operate in our homes. We are to elevate, raise, and lift our spouses. They should be higher than us. Our desire is to reveal to them our thoughts. We think they are more important than I am. They are the king/queen and I am a loyal subject.

You show honor by speaking honor. Words to and about your husband/wife ought to carry honor and respect. We often tell our children, "See your mom (dad)? That is the most important person on this planet." Denise constantly praises who I am. She will say things like, "Your father is one of the wisest people I know." She will share success stories from my life or ministry with them, accompanied by some word of honor lifting me up. We should also speak honor to each other. Do not assume she knows you respect her. Tell her. Point out character traits and things in her life which impress you. Tell her how awesome she is.

Honor is spoken, and it is an action. One way we seek to honor Denise in our home is by opening doors for her and carrying things instead of her. I jokingly tell the children, "Your mother is allergic to door handles, grocery bags, and suitcases. She should never touch them." If I am with her, I open her door. I get out of the car and walk to her door to open it and let her out. The only time I do not do this is when one of our kids beat me to it. It is a family value. Mom does not open doors or carry things. Denise is more than capable of doing these things. We show her honor by doing them for her. We also show her honor by giving her the best of everything. If I cook burgers, she gets the hottest and juiciest. If there is only one scoop of ice cream, she gets it. She gets the comfy chair and the back massage. Show your children by constant small actions your spouse is to be honored and respected. Show your husband/wife the same thing by doing it.

When our children were little, we had a disciplinary system we applied. I would discipline the kids if the offense occurred in front of me or if they disobeyed my instructions. Denise would do the same. The parent who was disobeyed merited the necessary discipline. There was one exception.

If the offense was one of disrespect, then both parents became a part of the correction. If a child was disrespectful to me, Denise would jump in and take over. She would tell them explicitly and then, with punishment, that I was worthy of respect and honor. She then made them come to me and ask forgiveness for not showing me honor. I did the same for her. The kids knew we respected each other and demanded it from them. They might get away with something with me, but I would not allow them to do it with their mom.

Honor is a verbal, and actual elevation of the other person, and it is for both spouses. It is seen and heard by the one receiving the honor and those around them. I read a book once which taught men are to love their wives and the wives respect their husbands. This is true. However, it is a two-way street. Men are to love and respect their wives. Women are to love and respect their husbands. It is to be tangible and felt. The actual test of honoring your spouse is this: Do they know it? Do they feel respected? Can they feel and see your respect? If they do not know you are honoring them, then you are not. In marriage counseling, many times I will ask one of the partners in front of the other. "Does he respect you for who you are?" I stop the other from answering and we listen to the one I asked. Often, there is a surprise. The person I asked will hesitantly answer they do not believe they are respected. The other one cannot believe it. My point is straightforward. If the one receiving respect and honor does not know it, then it isn't there.

Live in harmony with one another (Romans 12:16).

I am not a musician. My dad always said I could not carry a tune in a bucket. He also said I sang like a prisoner. I found myself behind a few bars and could not find the right key.

However, I love music. Harmony in music is the same as it is in a relationship. In a symphony, harmony happens when distinct notes from different instruments are brought together in a way that allows each one to complement and complete the other. Harmony is not unity. Harmony doesn't happen if a lot of the same instruments play the same note in the same manner. It happens when individual differences connect as a whole. They join forces and strengthen the overall work. A sound technician at my church told me how to tell if we had a good mix.

"Listen to the music, both instruments and vocals. Now, look at one particular instrument or singer. If you focus on them, you should be able to pick their instrument or voice out of the mix, but only if you try. If you do not try to hear them as separate individuals, then you hear the total as a whole. A good mix puts all the parts in harmony without canceling any individual."

Harmony in a relationship, especially a marriage, teaches we are not in competition with each other. Instead, we are in completion with each other. We are to complement the other person. We are their 'helper'. If they have a weakness, I am to apply my strength to it. Our marriage is a beautiful love song and God has designed it so our different lives harmonize together. We should not be arguing over differences, whether of opinion or memory.

We should seek to complete and fulfill each other. When my life can complement and strengthen the wife of my life, the result is our marriage and family is better.

In order to live in harmony, we must understand each other. I cannot complement my wife if I do not know her. Musically, the person arranging the musical piece is a master. They know how each instrument sounds and their strengths and weaknesses. They know how to blend a brass with the strings while a touch of percussion supports the piece. They must know the unique and individual instrument in order to bring a harmonious symphony to life. In our marriage, we must know each other. This reinforces spending time with each other. As we are together, we learn about each other. It also goes back to communication. I reveal to you who I am and you reveal to me who you are. We live in harmony when we utilize the strength of the other person to build the relationship as a whole.

I also must allow the other person to play a major part in my life if we are to live in harmony. This is not a solo with an occasional backup voice. You need to know you cannot become who God called you to become without your spouse. You need them to do their part in your life. You are dependent upon each other. Your spouse does not just complement who you are as in individual. They complete you. We must live in acknowledgment of this truth. I need Denise. Denise needs me.

I used music. Now I want to use art. When you view art, you see the finished product. You see the picture the artist painted. It isn't until you focus you see the individual colors, brush strokes, and blends. This is because the purpose of the artist was to bring all of these individual parts together into one image. We are the image of God. Male and female join together to complete the image of God created in the garden. Our marriage is to be an illustration, an image of the love Christ has for the church. We live together in harmony in order to show that image of Jesus Christ to the world. We are not married singles. We are a couple. We are one. I blend into her and she into me. Together, our one-flesh relationship harmonizes and glorifies Christ.

A great example in our lives is this. Denise is an analyst. She focuses on a task or decision and holds it up so she can see every facet. She looks down the road as far as she can to discern consequences and reactions to each choice. She thinks of the impact specific decisions will have on others. She has a sign in the kitchen which says, "Hold on. I need to overthink this."

I, on the other hand, make split decisions. Malcolm Gladwell wrote about my style in his book, Blink. I see a few choices and then just choose one of them. My basic metric is simple. If I am wrong, I will do something else next time. I tell the kids, "There are only three choices in life you cannot undo. Marriage. Pregnancy, and Jesus. So don't get hung up on lesser things." I am not sure if that is great advice, but it is advice none the less.

Often Denise will ask my opinion and I will almost instantly give it to her. Real life example is this. We were in the States and going to visit her mom. Denise decided to take a present and knew her mom liked a particular style of shirt. We went to the store.

Denise held up three different colors of the same basic shirt and asked, "Which one should I get?"

"Get the blue one." I said without hesitation.

"Why?" She wanted to know.

"Babe, I do not know. I have no definable reason. You asked. Blue popped into my mind, I said it." That was the only reason I could give.

She took about five minutes thinking through other shirts her mom wore, colors her mom liked, the current season or what was left of it, and a few more metrics before choosing the shirt. It wasn't the blue one.

The result is she always gives us the best gifts.

She plans the world's greatest vacations.

She makes wise decisions.

I understand this. I used to get frustrated over a ten-minute shirt color decision until I realized she invested this time in buying gifts for me as well. She invests time and thought into making decisions and I now understand she is better at making significant choices than I am.

Conversely my Ramen noodle, instant choice personality irritated her in our early years. She understood as she grew in love and in our relationship to rely on my quick decisions to get things done. Not every decision can take 20 minutes of analysis. She recently said she is impressed with how I can make decisions so quickly and that they are often the best one. She values the way I make decisions and I value the way she does. We both have our time and place. We have learned to not try and change the other one, but to appreciate what they offer the relationship. She depends on me for ordinary, every day, what we need to do decisions. I go to her for any heavy, weighted, significant determinations. I also let her buy the presents. We harmonize.

Build up one another (Romans 14:19; 1 Thessalonians 5:11).

Our words and actions are who we are. I will devote a chapter to communication, but in summary here let me say our words ought to improve the heart and emotions of our spouse. I mentioned this in the section on honor. Denise verbally honors me to me and to others. She speaks and shows honor. This phrase in Romans emphasizes the spoken word. We are to edify and lift, not tear down. I once commented in a sermon about a fellow pastor, David Janney. He has an ability to make me feel significant. Every time I talk to him, I leave the conversation feeling important. As I preached it, the Holy Spirit spoke to me and said, "Your wife should be able to say this about you."

I thought about that and prayed over it. Does Denise 'feel', and the key word is 'feel' important because of my words? How does your spouse feel after you speak to them? I know a couple who seek to give each other at least one sincere compliment a day. They try to find their spouse doing something well and speak to it. It is not empty flattery. It is sincerity.

He said, "I want her to know I see her. I know she is there and our lives are better because of her. I want her to hear from me how important she is. She serves the family. She blesses me. She ministers in the church. All the time she is there helping and doing and ninety-nine percent of the time, no one notices. We all just take her for granted. I want her to hear from me, at least once a day, I see her. I appreciate her. I respect her."

That is such good advice. We need to not honor in some classroom, ivory tower, knowledge manner. Honor is a field laboratory done in life. In the jungle, or in a village, when we need to build a fire, we follow the same process. We put some type of tinder down and light it. It is almost nothing. It is just a little, maybe as big as my little finger. We focus on it. As it flames, we nurture it by blowing gently and slowly adding a little more. The process continues until we have a large cooking and campfire. It started with a little spark, nurtured into a flame. Your spouse has these little potential sparks of greatness in them. Do you pour water on it, or do you fan it into a flame? Your words and actions will do one of the two.

I read a story about a state governor. He and his wife saw a friend from high school working in a job many would consider menial. The wife dated this man before dating her current husband. The governor said, "Where would you be if you would have married him instead of me?"

"Living in the Governor's Mansion with him. Where would you be?" She answered.

This humorous story speaks truth. Our words do not just build up emotionally. Words have power. God says life and death are in our tongue. One of the main themes of the book of Proverbs is how to speak. God named Himself, "The Word". Words have power.

I build my spouse up by speaking affirmation into their life. I find and verbally acknowledge success and effort. In the same manner as the people who seek to give at least one compliment per day, we need to do our best to speak life to our partners.

I have finished two books in a science fantasy series

written for my grandchildren. One of my characters is from a culture who greets each other with the phrase, "I see and hear you." I have the character do this to illustrate how important it is for us to acknowledge other people and give them our undivided attention. My character, Johan is his name, will not break eye contact when speaking to someone. He says to do so is to stop seeing them. The idea is you are so important to me that nothing else matters. Undivided attention is a way of building each other up.

We build up by speaking words of gratitude to each other. We let the other person know we see their work and it means something to us. We acknowledge their sacrifice. I heard a pastor say this to his children in front of his wife. "Your mother is the most capable and talented person I know. She is not one of, she is the one. She could do anything and do it successfully. She is brilliant. She could, if she wanted to, run a Fortune 500 company. She gave up her full ride scholarship in mathematics in order to stay home as my wife and your mom. She sacrificed worldly success and recognition out of her love and desire to serve us. She is incredible."

As he spoke to the children, I watched his wife. She seemed to grow two inches in height during his praise of her.

After my first term on the mission field, I returned to the States on a home assignment. My home church, where I was the pastor before leaving for Bolivia, had me there to preach. It was the first church I visited in the States. The pastor called me on the stage and said a lot of extremely nice and sincere things about me. Then, before I could preach, the church broke out in applause and then stood to their feet. I wept. It was so life affirming. It was so edifying. It was incredible.

This is how our spouses should feel. We need to build them up by acknowledging their work for us and the family. We also build them up by encouraging effort and growth. It isn't merely what they do, it is who they are seeking to become. Encourage each other verbally through the challenges and opportunities of life. Denise knew I wanted to be an author. During CoVid, when we were literally locked down in a Bolivian quarantine, she said, "You should write a book." Many times over the course of a few weeks she complemented my ability to communicate and encouraged me to write. She mentioned sermons and illustrations I used. As a direct result of her building me up, I am writing my eighth book. She saw something in me. It was a little spark. She gently nurtured it into a flame.

Building up your spouse happens when you realize you do not need to dim their light in order for yours to shine. It is the opposite. The brighter they shine, the better you are because of it. Too often, couples seem to look at each other as friendly competition. The success of one comes at the loss of the other. This isn't true. We are successful as long as either of us is successful. Build up your spouse. Encourage them. Speak life to them. Seek to be intentional in bringing out the greatness God has placed in them.

Be likeminded towards one another (Romans 15:5).

I will talk about this in the chapter on unity. Likeminded literally means to think in common. Our view of marriage and the purpose of our marriage ought to be the same. Our desires and dreams should coexist and complement each other. The idea is that of a roadtrip. Denise and I love taking roadtrips. In the car, it doesn't matter who is driving or who is in the passenger seat. It does not matter who chose the music or podcast on the radio. It doesn't matter whose turn it is to sleep. In the car, we both head the same direction at the same speed to the same destination. This is likeminded. We are going the same direction for the same purpose.

This doesn't mean we have the same opinions on everything all the time. A couple might disagree on many things. I know a couple where the husband is a staunch Libertarian and the wife belongs to a different political party. They vote for different candidates. Yet, they are likeminded in life and marriage. Some friends of ours have a marriage where the wife is a Calvinist, and the husband is not. They serve and worship Christ together. This is because likeminded doesn't mean the same. It means going the same direction. Likeminded common goals are what we should seek. We need to have a purpose for our marriage and seek to fulfill it. We listen to each other and develop a unified mindset about money, children, and other significant decisions. The way to do this is by letting the Word of God determine what we think and do. I recommend having literal, written goals for your marriage, family, and life. If you have a weekend to contemplate the next year and three years and establish family goals to strive for, it points both of you in the same direction. Many times, couples are not like-minded because they are pursuing different goals or purposes.

The first step to becoming truly likeminded is to understand your spouse. We need to stop assuming and start knowing. I will not be likeminded until I know what their mind is like.

The second step is to ensure our marriage is moving and we are both going the same direction. Many marriages struggle because one of the two begin a journey the other one is not a part of. A career choice is not simply the decision of the person with the job offer. It impacts all. So often in counseling, the root of the marriage problem is a decision made without the approval or encouragement of the spouse.

A missionary couple shared with us their story. The wife felt the call of the Holy Spirit to move to another country and work with evangelism among the villages. The husband did not share this call. They prayed. They talked. They sought counsel. The wife waited patiently as they served in the local church until one day about two years later, the husband said. "I am ready. God confirmed it with me. Let's go." Later on, as they looked back, the wife shares of all the things God did to prepare them during this two-year frame. They attribute a lot of their success on the mission field to what happened as they waited and grew until likemindedness occurred. Once more, we see the importance of communication and sharing with each other.

I witness the exact opposite happen on the mission field. A couple, or family, arrives excited and ready to serve. Unfortunately, either because they did not raise enough money, or due to having young children, one spouse is semi-stuck at home. The other takes language classes and is out in the community and culture. One's life is an adventure as they make new friends and experiences a new ministry. The other is under a type of house arrest and left behind.

One has direction and purpose. The other has more chores than ever. In sixteen years of living on the mission field, I know of seven missionary families who did not make it and I believe the reason is simple. He went one direction. She went another. We have to make sure we are not leaving our spouse behind in the excitement of new beginnings. Include one another in your process. You are both an essential part of the goal. It's not a goal for just one partner, it is a goal of the marriage.

We must understand each other and choose to travel in the same direction together. We have to develop common goals and discuss openly our thought processes. This leads us to likeminded living.

Accept one another (Romans 15:7).

God made us different. It is not just male and female. We are as different as our thumbprints. No two are the same. God gave us unique personalities. I am an sanguine Tigger. I bounce and bounce and bounce and bounce and have fun, fun, fun. My wife is a choleric Pooh. She is just happy to be here. We celebrate this. My Christmas stocking and coffee cup are Tigger. Hers are Pooh. I have Tigger pajamas. She has Pooh. In her phone, my contact name is Tigger. She is Pooh in mine. We constantly laugh about it and poke fun at each other. We both have unique talents and abilities. Neither is better than the other. Neither holds a higher esteem.

Many of you probably know couples whose childhood history and home values are radically different. By the providence of God, there is a high school friend who is now a missionary in Ghana. He lives in Accra. I live in Tamale. However, we do large evangelism events together and when he is here or I am there, we stay with each other, or at least eat together. He shares his testimony. He is from a broken home. His parents divorced after both committed adultery multiple times. He ended up living in the inner city while his mom was a bartender and then became a prostitute. He started drugs at age 11. By the time he was 15, three different schools kicked him out. He hated authority. He hated God. He hated life. He became a drug addict, dealer and alcoholic. God saved him as he sat jail one night as a teenager. His wife is the daughter of a missionary couple. Her dad is still a pastor. Her brother is a pastor. Her sister is married to a pastor. She attended church three times a week her entire young life and accepted Jesus in pre-school. She served and lived for Jesus her entire life.

Everything about their childhood is different. Their parents disciplined them and trained them differently. Their homes had different values. Their backgrounds are as different as night is from day, or darkness from light. They share how these backgrounds allow them to reach people for Christ. She can understand the good person who needs Jesus. He relates to the hard-hearted person who needs Jesus.

The Holy Spirit gifts people differently. He gives gifts to us in order to glorify Him in the church. Your spiritual gifts could be totally diverse. Friends of ours laugh at the prophetic gift of the wife married to the mercy gift of the husband. She wants to tell people how it is and shake the dust off her feet. He wants to hug them. Both are correct.

As you seek to grow into Christ-likeness and be likeminded, recognize and celebrate the uniqueness you have between yourselves. Celebrating differences allows us to experience the harmony we already spoke about. We do not let the differences of our spouse irritate us. They are who God made them to be. He did it because you need them. You need the person God uniquely crafted for the purpose of being your companion. Accept them. I already wrote about our two biggest differences. Denise is an over-thinker, and I am an under-thinker.

Sometimes in couple's therapy, I assign each person the task of writing down the top five qualities and abilities of their spouse. They also have to list more than one reason each of these qualities is a blessing to the marriage, with an example or story. This exercise causes many to appreciate their husband/wife with new insight. God created you to be different, yet indispensable to each other. This is how you accept each other. You understand and acknowledge God knew what He was doing when He created your spouse. He put you together for a purpose. You need them. They need you. You cannot be who God created and called you to be without their God-given influence, and neither can they.

Admonish one another (Romans 15:14; Colossians 3:16).

This is being proactive in encouraging and challenging each other to pursue God in a Spirit-filled fashion. I must be honest on this command of God. It is universally ignored in churches and marriages. The idea is simple. We want to discern where God is working in the life of our spouse and join the Holy Spirit as He seeks to work in their life. Word of warning. The temptation is to try to get the Holy Spirit to help us change our spouses or get them to do something we want. No. Admonition is seeing God at work and joining Him in blessing your spouse.

God gives husbands the example of doing this in Ephesians 5. He tells us we are to help present our wives as sanctified and holy before the Lord. The idea is we want to help them grown in their pursuit of Christ. It is not just for the man. It is for one-another. Encourage your spouse to take part in the church's life and be engaged in ministry. I gave my life to Christ in college. Denise's parents purchased a Bible and gave it to me. Denise recommended sermon tapes for me to listen to and discuss with her. I remember one day she came to me and said, "Starting next week, I serve in the four-year-old Sunday school class as a teacher. I think it would be wonderful if you served with me. You can connect with them through your ability to tell stories and personality."

I told her I did not know the Bible stories because of my childhood. We did not attend church. I did not know the stories. Her answer, "I can tell them to you and we can read them together. I really think you would be an awesome teacher."

That was over forty years ago. I have been a Bible teacher since the first Sunday in the four-year-old class where I taught about David and Goliath and had a little boy 'chop' off my head as I thrashed on the floor in a death worthy of an Oscar nomination. She admonished me then. She still does. We memorize Scripture together. One of my favorite early marriage memories are of the two of us quoting the Book of James in bed before going to sleep. We decided to memorize the entire book word perfect in 90 days. Each night I would start with chapter one, verse one and quote as far as possible. She did it afterwards. It is a precious memory.

We should admonish each other to pursue the revealed will of God. Talk to your spouses about their personal devotions. Ask them what God is doing in their life. How is God talking to them? What challenges do they face in obedience? How and where are they changing to become more like Jesus?

Admonish each other to share Christ in their circles. Ask for a list of names of their lost coworkers and friends so you can pray for them to come to Jesus. If you see an area God is working in the life of your husband or wife, let them know and encourage their growth. Challenge them to follow the Holy Spirit. Ask them about verses they are memorizing or passages they read. Let them know your goal is to help them grow in grace. I believe this is so important I incorporate it into my wedding vows when I perform a wedding. I do not have the typical, "Do you promise to love, cherish and obey?"

The vows I have each person repeat in pre-marriage counseling and during the actual ceremony is this.

"I vow to help you become the person God created you to be. I commit myself to working with the Holy Spirit and challenging you to follow Him. I promise before God and each other to admonish you to good works and God's glory."

How do you admonish each other? I listed it above. You

start off with the revealed will of God. Push each other to pursue Christ in their personal devotions, to serve in the local church, and to evangelize their friends. Then, as you share with each other how God is personally working in your life, become a loving accountability partner.

Care for one another (1 Corinthians 12:25).

Caring for each other comprises considerate actions of love. It is showing kindness and concern through thoughtful actions and gentle words. It is to nurture. The word is used in the husbandry of plants and the oversight of a pastor and their sheep. You focus on the needs of the one you care for.

This is a good example of my wife and I having unique gifts. I have a brown thumb. She has a green one. Denise can bring a dead plant to life and I can destroy acres of forest in a single night. One time she took a trip. A friend gave her a cactus plant for Christmas. She asked me to care for it during her trip. I killed it. I did not know you could kill cactus. I thought they were the roaches of the plant world. I assumed after the apocalypse the world would consists of nothing other than roaches eating cacti. I was wrong.

She came back and nurtured it to life. She told me husbandry was not a secret. All you have to do is to know the plant you care for. Does it need shade or sun? How much of each? Does it require a lot or a little water? Should it be facing north or south? Is it an inside or outside plant? She understands these things. Remember her being a research expert? She looks at the various plants throughout the house and in the yard and meets their particular needs.

She walked me through the house and yard and told me about each one. She knew what each plant needed to survive and thrive. You care for the plant through meeting its needs.

As parents, we care for our children. We even call it childcare. The idea is to meet the needs of the child in a safe environment. We understand the needs of a teen are not the same as those of an infant. Or we should. One thing we cover many times in our parenting conferences is this subject. As children grow, our care for them must change. We do not, or should not, parent a 16-year-old the same way we do a six-year-old. Their needs are different. It is our job to meet them at their point of need. As parents, we seek to nurture and care for our children through the various stages of life.

I put forth we need spouse-care. You care for your spouse the same way. Through conversation, research, communication and field work, you discern their needs. You then seek to meet their physical and emotional needs lovingly. You nurture each other. One time, many years ago, Denise came to me and told me she was about to have a breakdown. She was not speaking figuratively. I am high octane and run non-stop. We planted a church and during the summer we did various back-to-back events, outreaches, small groups and hosted mission teams to help us. She came to me after six weeks of non-stop activity and guests in our home. No exaggeration. Guest lived with us for over 42 days. I allowed ten people to stay with us for a week.

"I am done." She told me. "I am empty. I can do no more. I will go visit my parents in Texas for a few weeks until I can recharge."

I realized in my zeal to reach others for Christ, I hurt my wife. There were two more people planned to stay with us. A couple of friends and a relative's family were scheduled to use our home as a hotel while they visited the area. I called them and told them they had to change their plans. I told them they could not stay with us. I confessed my failure as a husband and took full responsibility. My lack of care was destroying my wife.

I wish I could say I learned my lesson that week. The truth is, several times in our marriage, I have not cared for her needs in this same manner. I recently took a short-term team to the airport. They spent ten days with us. I brought another team home on the same bus. They arrived on the flight the first team departed on. It exhausted Denise. It is not a strength of mine or a weakness of hers. It is our differences. I am learning. I try to schedule times of rest in between large events. The reason is I want to care for her. I want to help her.

We need to understand the needs of our spouses and how to help them grow. In the example of plants I used above, the ones who need a lot of sunlight are not better than plants which need shade. They are different. Caregiving happens as we meet the needs of the individual. Spouse-care happens as I understand what my spouse needs and then meet it. Both are essential. I comprehend who my spouse is, who God created them to be, how they are wired and what they need. I then do my best to meet that need. They have emotional needs. They have relational needs. They have physical needs. They have spiritual needs. We must know them holistically and meet their needs.

Serve one another (Galatians 5:13).

Caring for each other is meeting needs. This goes one step beyond that. You don't merely seek to meet needs. You search for ways to express love by giving your spouse thoughtful service. Denise does not really care about shopping. When it is gift-giving time, she loves it. She loves to look for just the right gift. However, chore shopping is literally a chore for her. I discovered this many years ago. I do almost all the task-oriented shopping in our house. The thing is this. She knows I also dislike it. I do it as a gift of service to her. It is not a huge thing, but it serves her and lets her know I love her. Think about how little this is. I buy the milk and bread for the family. It isn't the size of the task. It is the motivation behind it. Do some act of service for your spouse just to say "I love you" without using words.

I know of a couple where the wife loves to receive a massage. We drank coffee one night and as we talked; she shared with us a gift he gave her over a year ago. She came home and discovered he purchased a massage table, warming blanket, oils, and lotions. He also had a book on how to give massages. Every Wednesday night for a year, he gave her a one hour massage. He still gives her one once or twice a month. They bought a new table because the old one broke through being used so much. This one hour time investment and small outlay of cash meant the world to the wife.

A man shared a small act his wife did for him. He typically arrived home from work the same time each day.

She greets him at the door with a deep kiss and a cup of decaf coffee. They sit on the couch and talk for ten minutes. It is a time to decompress. There are no chores to do. They do not talk about tasks or errands. They chat. Nothing more. He said it is a beautiful transition from work to home and makes him feel welcomed and loved.

This is what it means to serve one another. Find an area where your spouse could use a boost or help. It can be of the heart, head, or action. You find it and do it.

Bear one another's burdens (Galatians 6:2).

Serving each other is a proactive showing of care and love. Bearing each other's burdens is reactive. In life, we will get hit and sometimes hit hard. The best (worst) example I can think of is when my 29-year-old son died. It hit me hard. I found it difficult to function. I do not know what I would have done without Denise carrying me. She helped me shoulder the burden of grief. She allowed, rather encouraged me, to grieve. She took me to a Grief Share class/group, and we did the work together. For the first year after he passed, she was there to hold me and help me with no imposed expectations on how I should grieve or when I ought to be at some other grief phase. She just carried the weight. I was free to be weak and broken because she would put her arm around me and help me keep limping forward. That is bearing one another's burdens.

She carried my burden. As I type this, it has been four years since he went to heaven. Yesterday we talked about another couple who currently are experiencing some heavy stress, or the wife is. We told the man, "You need to humble yourself and do your best to pick her up and serve her. This is marriage and Christian living. She needs you. Now. She needs you. Be there for her."

Afterwards I told Denise, "It reminds me of when Seth died. In our marriage, I am Tigger. I am bouncy and fun. I do not get depressed. I am the eternal optimist. When he died, you let me crash and caught me. You were okay with me not being upbeat. You let me grieve. You let me be sad. You let me hurt. You did not judge. You did not try to teach me. You let me cry in your arms and fall asleep on you. You carried my burden."

Four years later, her doing that for me is one of the most significant things which has happened in my life. Consider this. We use the words carry one another's burden a lot in the Christian world, but consider momentarily what carrying a burden is. When it is a burden, a load, a weight your spouse carries with you, they are working. Carrying weight is work. Not easy work. Hard work. It is a struggle. It is especially difficult when you are both hurting from the same circumstance. It is a significant emotional event. Serving one another by carrying as much of the load as you can is life and relationship changing. It is the example of Jesus going to the cross to carry our sins for us. It is huge.

Be patient with one another (Ephesians 4:2; Colossians 3:13).

In our marriage relationship, we will irritate each other. We have distinct personalities. The same things which require us to live in harmony often tempt us to discord. Instead of a symphony, we end up with noise. We respond differently to various events and have many unexpressed expectations. The opportunity to become angry with each other is daily. The word patience is specifically regarding this. We are to joyfully let slight irritations roll off of us. We do not get angry because anger happens when we dam up the emotions and they overflow. Patience opens the spillway and lets the things which lead to anger leave us. When you have patience with someone, there is no buildup. Patience is like throwing a feather into a bottomless pit. You will never fill the pit. It is like throwing a match into the lake. There is nothing to catch on fire, and the lake actually extinguishes the small flame. I believe this is the root of patience. It refused to keep score. True patience doesn't just 'take it' from the other. It transforms you.

In counseling, more than once, one of the couple will say, "I have been patient, but my patience is coming to an end." I let them know this means they are not patient. They pretended to be on the outside, but they have kept a running account of every wrong on the inside. I take them to 1 Corinthians 13 where love is patient and does not keep an account of a wrong suffered. We look at Galatians 5 and see patience is a fruit of the Holy Spirit.

Patience is new every single time it is needed. It is not a pothole in the road which slowly fills up, one little pebble at a time. It is the grand canyon. Patience is a proactive character. It is not from you. It is to you. I do not need patience if you are not irritating me. I am to be patient with you. God is working in your life and He is working in my life through you. That includes this moment.

Speak the truth in love (Ephesians 4:15, 25).

The context of this passage is not one of confronting someone. This verse has been used to justify tactless and even harsh speech. Christians use it to feel good about being mean on social media. Let's talk about speaking the truth. Since we love our spouse, and our fellow Christian, we will not lie to them. On the surface, this sounds easy, but how many times have either of you misled your spouse? How many times have you allowed your spouse to believe something untruth because it served you? My wife asked me to get the mail on the way home. I forgot. Later on I heard her tell our daughter, who had mailed us a package, "Dad checked the mail today and we have not received it." I did not correct her. So, was it a lie? I believe any type of deception and falsehood fits into this admonition of speaking only the truth out of our love for each other. I did not admit my failure for purely selfish reasons.

We seek to teach our kids the value of complete honesty. When they begin to date, we have three basic rules. One of them is do not allow any deception of any kind. We say, "If a group of youth are going to a movie, and your heart throb is with them. Do not ask if you can hang out with your friends when your purpose is to be with that one specific person….and your friends will be there also. Ask if you can go see him/her and let us know other people will be there. If they are the main reason you want to go, don't let us assume another reason. Do not allow deception to happen."

Deceptions are contrary to love, which does not seek its own. Our husband/wife needs to have the full confidence of our integrity and truthfulness in everything all the time. It is a real life application of Jesus when He said, "Let your yes be yes and your no be no." Your spouse can rest in total confidence of absolute honesty. I think a great way to think of this verse is: Because of your love, always say the truth.

Be kind and compassionate to one another (Ephesians 4:32).

Do you notice how many of these one-another admonitions have to do with visually, verbally and in action expressing our love? Imagine your relationship with your spouse if you were always on the lookout for some way to express love to him/her!

Kindness is an action motivated by the need, emotionally or physically, of someone. It is proactively helping them.

I had a friend tell me. "Whenever we go to the store, we tell our children we have a goal. We want to be the nicest and kindest person the cashier interacts with today. We speak to them. We complement them. We encourage them. We want to leave them with a smile on their face, no matter how big a frown they possessed when we arrived."

That is kindness. We wrongly changed kindness from an action into an ambivalent character quality. We refer to people as kind, but never as doing kind. In a small group of pastors drinking coffee during a break, one pastor pointed to someone not in the group with us and said, "Do you know Pastor Paul? He is literally one of the kindest people I have ever met." I do not know why, but I asked, "What makes you say that? What kindness does he do?" It was a legitimate question, and the answer was a blank stare and silence. Can you be kind without action? What is kindness if it has no object who actually receives it? In our marriage, we are to be kind to each other. It is like caring for each other but with a gentle heart attitude. Kindness creates a picture of smiling humility in my mind. I am happy to do this for you because I know you need it.

Compassion literally means 'to suffer together'. It focuses on empathy. I am not seeking a level of relationship with my wife which only allows me to see her pain. I want to go deep enough to understand it as much as I can, and to share her pain and help her carry it. Compassion calls for an understanding of the other person and leads to merciful and gracious acts of love. These are connected in this passage because true compassion will lead to acts of kindness. When I feel your pain, I will seek to ease it. With words and with actions.

I shared my story of brokenness earlier. Denise did not just let me grieve. She entered into my world and did it with me. Now, after going through this, we can help other people through suffering together. Our pain and sorrow allow us to not just understand, but feel the pain and sorrow of another. In God's timing, my wife received this last night. I did not know today I would write this chapter. I simply had time, so I started expanding my notes. Last night Denise received this from a woman we do not know. Her teenage son suddenly died because of an infection. She is a Christian and someone told her of our story.

"Denise, when you get a chance, could you please share you experience with me. I really need some help right now. I am overrun with guilt and blaming myself for his death… I feel like I let him die....everything went wrong and I will never get over this. Pray that God helps me, please."

Denise does not have words to say, she has understanding. Nothing she can say will help this mom. Denise can help her with compassion. Denise understands and feels her pain and this woman realizes that. She reached out, not for advice, but for love. This is compassion. Denise shares compassion when she shares with this woman and empathizes with her pain.

We are to show compassion to each other. I am to try and enter into the world of my wife and feel her pain. I do not have to solve it and I certainly should not say that she shouldn't feel that way. So often we need a hug and compassion, and people give us advice or dismiss our feelings. Be compassionate with each other.

Submit to one another (Ephesians 5:21, 1 Peter 5:5).

This is the twin of honoring the other. When I honor you, I lift you up as more important than myself. Submission is joyfully submitting my will to you. It is acknowledging we are equal, but I want to place my own desires below yours.

I once had a wife tell me, "I have no trouble submitting to him if he agrees with me." She said that with a straight face. I taught them this is the opposite of submission. That is doing what you want to do. You are not submitting if your submission was your desire all along.

We teach our children submission is "doing the will of my authority with the same joy and attitude as my will. It is doing what I don't want to do with the same passion as doing my own personal choice."

If I want to do something and my wife wants something else, submitting to her is doing what she wants to do with the same attitude I would have done my choice. It is not begrudgingly giving in to them. It is joyfully allowing them the choice. Most of the time, neither one of us knows the other person submitted. I just think she wanted to do this all along. The truth is, she wanted to do something else. Her submission caused me to think she wanted my way. A good illustration is the elder board at my church. We agree to maintain a united front. More than that, to maintain unity. We will discuss a topic. Some of us may be more or less passionate than the others. The result is this. When we make a decision, the entire elder board owns it. We tell no one in the church, "The elders voted for this. I didn't, but I was not in the majority." Instead, the elder who may have been outvoted joyfully surrenders to the will of the board and communicates the unified will. In a marriage, we joyfully surrender our will and our rights to the service of the marriage and the other. It is never done with a pout. It is always a joy.

Denise and I talked about a vacation. I wanted to go on a cruise, actually two cruises. I wanted to do one with the children and then another without them. Back-to-back cruises. She took off with the idea and researched it. Her super power of frugality and deal finding combined with her genetically enhanced decision-making ability allowed her to find the perfect cruises. We ended up going on them both for less than one of the first ones I looked at. It was on the last night of our childless cruise she said, "I am glad we did this instead of rent an AirBnb." I did not know what she meant and pressed her on it. It was a slip of the tongue. I found out she did not want to go on a cruise. She wanted a different vacation. She researched AirBnb's and planned on surprising me. Then, she saw how much I wanted this, so she submitted her plans to mine. I never knew it. Her passion in research and planning made me forget it was my idea to take a cruise. She poured every ounce of energy and enthusiasm into "my" vacation as she did "her" vacation. I believe it is a beautiful image of true submission. Submission, when done with the right heart attitude, is practically invisible.

Consider others better than yourselves (Philippians 2:3).

This is contrasted to pursuing our own selfish ambition. This truly is a heart issue. It is like what I tell people in premarital counseling. "When we get married, nothing is ever about me. That is upside down thinking. WE replaces ME. My ambition is no longer the driving passion of my life. It is our ambition and your ambition. I am here to serve us by serving you."

This command is directly tied to the incarnation, life, and death of Christ. He chose this life of humility, even to death on the cross, because He chose us. There is no way in all of creation or eternity that we are in any minuscule way better than Jesus, yet He treated us as if we were better than Him. He laid down His very life for ours. It wasn't an even trade.

In our marriage, we need to intentionally view the spouse as the more important one. This is much more difficult than it sounds. Do you really view your spouse as better than yourself? Are her/his goals the ones we seek to accomplish?

This is a close relative of both honoring and submitting. Those are actions. This is an attitude. It is serving the other because you believe they are worthy of your service. I once read, "You know you are a servant by the way you react when treated like one." In this scenario, you do not mind it. You honor them and submit to them, and really believe you married up and out of your league. I, before God can testify to you, I do not deserve Denise. She is so much more than me in every way. I am little league, pee-wee division. She is all-pro. I am convinced this is a truth. I consider her better than me.

Pray for one another (James 5:16).

I have two confessions to make. The first is how shocked I am at the fact that most couples do not pray for each other. I do not mean pray with each other. I mean exactly what I said. We do not pray for each other. It shocks me.

The second confession is how little I pray for my wife. I pray. I pray a lot. I just, in the past, rarely prayed FOR her. If something were amiss I would, but other than those crisis moments, I almost never did. I am commanded to pray for her. I need to lift her to the throne constantly. So do you.

We need to pray for our husbands/wives to bear fruit. We need to ask God to work in their lives. We should pray for their growth and strength to overcome temptations. Pray for victory and wisdom. I once thought. "What if the growth of my wife depended on my prayers for her?" If you understand prayer at all, then you know this is not a hypothetical or rhetorical question. Her growth depends on prayer, my prayer. My growth is dependent and/or tied to her prayer. Pray for each other. All the time. Praying for someone connects your heart to them.

Once, when I first became a Christian, there was a man in our church who I simply did not like. No explanation for my feelings. Denise recommended I pray for him. I put him on my daily prayer list and not long afterwards discovered he was a pretty decent guy and we became, and still are, friends. God used my prayers to change me, not him. God changed me so I could love better. This happens when you pray, daily pray, for each other.

I take this experience in my life and give this assignment to people in counseling. I ask them to pray for God's best for their husband/wife for at least 15 minutes a day. If they are the only person you pray for, fine. Pray for them, thank God for them, lift up their needs and desires before God. Do it sincerely for 15 minutes. The only limitation is you cannot pray for them to change into what you desire. Your goal is prayer cover, support and cooperation with God. Pray for them.

In all the times I assigned this, not once did a couple complete it. How can it be so difficult to pray for each other? It is due to spiritual warfare. Satan knows God uses your prayers. If you pray for him/her, then God will work in their life, your life and your marriage. God will do it. Yes He will!

Pray for each other. Pray with each other, yes. Then, pray for each other.

Stop for a moment and look back at this list.

Love one another

Forgive one another

Be devoted to one another

Honor one another above yourselves

Live in harmony with one another

Build up one another

Be likeminded towards one another

Accept one another

Admonish one another

Care for one another

Serve one another

Bear one another's burdens

Be patient with one another

Speak the truth in love

Be kind and compassionate to one another

Submit to one another

Consider others better than yourselves

Pray for one another

Imagine what your marriage would be like if you applied these principles. We will see how these apply to sex as well, but I want to reiterate. I have never encountered a great relationship who had a poor sex life, nor have I seen a great sex life with a poor relationship. If your marriage was full of love, thoughtfulness, forgiveness, kindness, compassion, humility, submission, passion, etc., how deep and profound would it be? This is God's will for your marriage. It is His stated plan.

Best Fellowship Forever Reflection Questions

1. Why is it that being alone and together interferes with what we think is 'getting things done'. Based on your actual past actions, what is more important than your spouse?

2. How often do you and your spouse do 'nothing' together? No agendas. No tasks to complete. No projects to finish. How often are you simply with each other because you love each other?

3. Joe said he often hears Denise say, "You are here, but you are not HERE. Where are you?" Do you discover yourself thinking of other things when you are with each other, but not thinking of each other when you are doing other things?

4. One of the purposes of marriage is to complete each other. We are to be unified. It is hard to be one if you are always need to be in two places. It is hard to be one if you are always doing two separate things. Do you find yourselves trying to do more and living with such little margin in life you don't have time for each other?

5. Rate yourself and your spouse in these 'One Anothers' of Scripture. Do not let your partner see your self-evaluation or your evaluation of them. Now, switch and look at what the other person said both about you and them. Talk about it. Remember, this is their PERCEPTION. It might not agree with

yours and it might not be accurate. However, this is how they perceive the relationships. Rather than argue, seek to discern what led them to this conclusion or to a different conclusion than yours. 0 is the worst and 10 is the best. Rate yourself first. Then rate your spouse.

1. Unconditional love.
2. Unconditional and instant forgiveness.
3. Be devoted.
4. Honor above yourself.
5. Live in harmony.
6. Build each other up.
7. Be likeminded.
8. Accept one another.
9. Admonish one another.
10. Care for one another.
11. Serve one another.
12. Bear the other's burdens.
13. Be patient.
14. Speak truth in love.
15. Be kind and compassionate.
16. Submit to each other.
17. Consider the other better than yourself.
18. Pray for each other.

Intentional And Spontaneous

A great relationship takes work.

I always hated that statement. I planned on writing a book titled, Marriage Takes Work and have the word "Work" crossed out with "Love" written over it.

I don't like it when friends post on social media something like: "Happy anniversary to my wife. It hasn't always been easy and not always fun, but so happy we committed to each other." Anything in that vein I did not like. It makes it look like a great marriage is a pain in the bottom. It is worth it and it is good; however, the only way to have a great relationship is to do your time, punch the clock, put in the work, and hopefully get a payday worth it.

It makes marriage seem almost like a necessary evil.

Marriage is work.

Work is not fun.

Therefore, marriage is not fun.

That is the logic it seemed to communicate to me.

I changed my mind. Marriage takes work. I just want to redefine the term. Work is extended energy. I looked up the word in a few dictionaries and to paraphrase them all, work is engaging in physical and/or mental activity in order to accomplish a desired result. That is the work which I reference. It isn't working in the sense of a Genesis 3 curse. It isn't work in the hard drudgery of life. It is not work as a four letter word.

It is focused effort and expended energy to reach a desired goal. Your goal is a fulfilling love relationship which illustrates the very love of God to the world. Your goal is creating the happiest place on earth. Your goal is being married to your best friend and enjoying great sex and intimacy. It is a goal worth putting effort into achieving.

A great relationship must be intentional. The laws of physics apply to relationships as well. Motion takes effort. Atrophy happens without work. Relationships slow down, stop, and then stagnate. Growth is like riding your bike up a huge hill. If you stop pedaling, you will stop gaining. The most you can hope for is to not go downhill. Climbing means work.

We have to put the effort into our relationships if we want to reach our goals. Marriage must be intentional. I think many relationships are like the famous words of the lost pilot. "I do not know where I am heading, but I am getting there at a high rate of speed." Moving is not the same thing as going somewhere. You could be like a hamster in a wheel, busy at work, but not going anywhere, or worse than just moving, you might be headed somewhere you do not want to end up at.

I love Andy Stanley. I think he is insightful and a fantastic teacher. He taught a series called the Principle of the Path. I 'baptized' it into my own little world and taught it at my church. My congregation thinks I am pretty smart, thanks to Andy. He will forgive me. He has to. He taught on forgiveness as well. That is beside the point. I am giving him the credit for this. He has an overarching principle. Here it is. Direction determines destination. I now say this all the time. Direction determines destination. It is true in geography. I am writing this while on a layover at Miami International Airport. If I decided I wanted to rent a car and drive to New York, what would happen if I jumped in it and sped off to the south? Would I arrive in Manhattan in time to catch a Broadway play? What if I took off east as fast as my rented minivan could go? Or west? Would I arrive in New York City by driving in any of those three directions? No. What if I did not know better and truly believed New York was south of Miami? Would I arrive in New York because I believed I would? What if I had sincere motivations and a pure heart? What if I were rich? What if I were poor? Old? Young?

The only way I can arrive in New York is to head in the direction of it. It is my direction which determines my destination. This is true in geography. It is also true in finances. I will not become financially free if I continue in the direction of financial bondage. If the direction of my money management is that of spending more than I make and living on consumer debt, then the destination of my finances will not be financial freedom. I will end up in financial bondage since bondage is the destination of my direction.

It is true in my marriage. If I want to have an intimate, Christ honoring, enjoyable and fruitful marriage, then I must head in the direction which culminates in that destination. I cannot ignore the needs of my wife, never communicate with her, treat her unkindly and take her for granted, and then arrive at the city of intimacy. I cannot put my career and children over my wife for 25 years and wake up her best friend. I cannot ignore intimacy and arrive at a great sex life. My direction determines my destination.

This is part of being intentional. I addressed this in the section on likeminded. We are to be like-minded with one another. We need to determine both the destination we want to arrive at and the steps to get there. We need goals and evaluation of them.

Goals in our relationship give us a direction to grow as well as a metric to measure our growth. Think about it. How do you determine in your marriage whether you are growing? How do you measure your relationship? A goal is a tool to allow us to do that. It lets us see if we are moving and, if so, what direction we are traveling. Goals can define success for us. It moves that word, success, from an ideal into a measurable activity.

Goals in our relationship allow us to be proactive. If we are not intentionally proactive, we are unintentionally reactive. Someone is determining our direction and our destination. If it is not you, then who is it? I once heard of a Stanford Business study of the top 5% of the Forbes 500 executives. These high octane achievers had one thing in common. They all had written goals to give them direction and destination. The principles which allow for success in the marketplace, boardroom and corporate entities work for relationships also.

We need to have written goals in our relationship. We agree these are our targets. When Denise and I first married, we established written goals for one, three, and five years. We achieved them all. Now, almost 39 years later, we still function with goals.

Right now we are, and as of this sentence, it is still unannounced, moving to Ghana. (We are now here, but I wrote this chapter before and it is a good illustration so I left it in the book). We believe God has called us to go from Bolivia, where we served the last 15 years, to West Africa. We have a goal of serving there at least 10 years. We set up little goals as we transition our ministries and hand them off to our Bolivian friends. We have set goals for our move from Bolivia. We are building a house in Ghana. It is a small little cinder block one, but we are designing it now with the goal of having it built before we arrive there in five months. I am on a trip to the States and one of the things I am doing in my travel time is establishing fundraising goals. We need monthly support and upfront monies to establish our home and ministry there. We set communication goals for informing our current donors. We have research goals, team building goals, ministry goals, financial goals, and relationship goals. We had to discuss the education of the last two kids at home, Patience and Mercy. We set goals for them. Patience will finish high school in Africa, so we made goals for her to begin on-line college shortly after we arrive.

I just rattled that last paragraph off. It flowed from my fingertips. These are just some goals we have. I will turn 60 years old the same year we move to West Africa. I do not plan on retiring in the sense of the word. I do know age will cause me to slow down. Yesterday, while driving, Denise and I talked about our future and finances. There were options and plans discussed. We need to formalize our discussion into a 10-year plan with a defined financial goal at the end. We will do that. It will probably happen within the next two weeks.

How much expended energy in order to reach a desired outcome occurs in your marriage? We need the desired outcome. This is a goal. It needs to be discussed and agreed upon. It should be written down.

That last sentence is important. A goal is not a goal unless it is in writing, so you and/or others can see it. It is just an idea until you put it on paper. You articulate better on paper. You see exactly what it is you hope to accomplish. Let me give you some ideas on how to do this.

First, write out in one complete sentence what your goal is. The sentence should be as concise as possible while fully stating the desired outcome. This means you thought through the goal enough to summarize it. One sentence is smaller than a tweet. The two of you discuss your desires and dreams. Communicate expectations and hopes. After fully understanding each other, write it down.

Now, agree upon a deadline to accomplish it. A goal without a date is nothing more than a dream. A deadline makes it real. Your goals should be difficult to attain, but with hard work and discipline do-able, and you should be able to do it by a particular date. Do not say, "We will talk more." That is a desire. Write this. "By January of 2023, we will spend no less than 30 minutes a day in uninterrupted conversation about our lives." This makes your 'talking more' quantifiable and establishes a date to accomplish it. In 1986, I surrendered to the ministry and we felt I needed college and seminary. We established this goal. "I will complete my undergraduate degree by the end of 1990 and will do it debt free." A second and related goal was this. "I will finish seminary debt free before December of 1993 with a GPA of no less than 3.5." These goals gave us definite direction. We were going into full-time ministry and had a time frame to accomplish it.

Direction determines destination. Remember that. It is not your goal. It is whether you are moving in the direction of your goal. So, break the goal down into steps. We took the educational goals I just shared with you and then broke down how to accomplish them. It included how many hours of school I took as well as our financial situation to let me do it debt free. We put together a seven-year plan. I graduated seminary in May of 1993 with a 3.52 gpa. I attained both my undergraduate and graduate degrees with no student debt or loans.

Establish your destination and then plan your direction. Start with a definite goal and then working backwards. Develop your plan using each step and giving it a date to accomplish. I start from the end and work backwards. I imagine myself with the goal accomplished and then ask what had to happen for this to take place? I write every task that I can think of and then put them in chronological order. A great example is in building. Builders use a project plan, not just a blueprint. The blueprints and the final concept are the goal. The project plan gives us the steps in order to accomplish it. I have to do the work on the site before I can roof the building. I have to put the pipes in underground before I paint the walls. I have to frame the building after I pour the concrete. When I pour the concrete, I have to wait a certain amount of time for it to dry before building on it. The walls have to hold the weight of the roof. They think about every step. It would be hard to put in the electrical cables at the end of the job. They have to do in before you use sheetrock and paint. In your tasks, look at the order you need to do them.

When Denise and I moved to Colorado to plant a church, we had a goal. "My church will have its first service in thirteen weeks, with over 100 people in attendance." In order to accomplish it, we imagined the Monday after our first service and then wrote everything which had to happen to make 'yesterday' a success. We ended up with a task list of more than 300 activities. Each task had a date, and we put it in order. We had our first service 13 weeks after moving to Denver. We started with no one on our team and had over 130 people in 13 weeks!

Goals have power. They motivate you. I truly believe a goal pulls you toward it. Set goals in your marriage. We have vacation goals. We have financial goals and parenting goals. These goals allow us to expand focused energy to attain a desired result. Set spiritual goals such as prayer time and scripture memory as a couple. We have a goal with our children that we will take them on a short-term mission trip. We are missionaries and we do this. Do it as a couple. Establish a goal to do short-term missions together every other year, or even every year. Set goals to do fun activities together. Make growth goals, such as attending a marriage seminar annually.

What do you desire in your marriage?

What are you doing to make it a reality?

I will speak more to this in the chapter on time management and living our values.

I cannot leave this chapter on being intentional without speaking to another side of it. Be intentionally spontaneous. This sounds like an oxymoron or trying to connect two opposites. It is not. They are not opposites because they are on different metrics. You can not be intentional without being spontaneous. Living unintentionally simply means allowing other people and circumstances to determine where you go in life and relationships. Living without focus is not the same thing as being spontaneous.

Your marriage is a living and breathing relationship. I

wholeheartedly believe in goal setting and living with a purpose. However, your marriage is not a business with a strategic plan. It is the union of two souls, knit together for life…and enjoyment. Learn to go with the flow at the moment. Spontaneous is to just do something suddenly, without premeditation. Intentional living is the basic ingredient of a good marriage and spontaneity is the spice that gives it flavor. Spice things up. I will talk some about this in our section on sex. However, it applies to just life in general. We have all heard of "seize the day". I say, "Grab the moment!"

More than once, Denise and I have gone on a date and decided to not go home. The first time it happened, we were driving home after going to the movie. We saw an Embassy Suites hotel. Embassy Suites is the hotel where we spent our first night as a married couple. We were married and our honeymoon flight was the next day, so we stayed our wedding night in an Embassy Suites near the airport. Not the one we saw. We were in Virginia and we got married in Texas. We saw the hotel, and it brought up our wedding night. We laughed about our bumbling sex and I told her, "I would do much better now."

"Really? Prove it." She said.

I turned the car around, and we went into the hotel. We called the kids and told them we would not be home. No luggage, no spare clothes, no preparation. We just spontaneously stopped and re-enacted our wedding night, only I did much better. (She said so).

We have done this several other times. We make little money, but we budget it and have a high value goal of great vacations. So, we save in order to spend money on vacations. One time I had five days off work because of a factory re-tooling. They had to change things up on the assembly line at General Motors, where I worked through college and seminary. We ate dinner and Denise said, "Let's go to Jamaica." The next day, we were on the plane. One Christmas Day we left her parent's house in Arlington, Texas after spending the holiday with them. On the way home, we talked about New Orleans and the French Quarter. As we talked, I turned the car to head east on the freeway. Our house was west. Denise did not notice it for about fifteen minutes. Then she said, "Where are you going?" I answered, "New Orleans." She looked at me. "Okay, sounds good."

We spent three days in a dump of a motel on the outskirts of town, since it was all we could afford. We would spend all day walking around the city and then go back to the cesspool of a hotel at night. It was awesome.

I mentioned at the beginning how many, I believe most, Christians allow their homes and marriages to become simply business. Now, I am telling you to make goals, set deadlines and manage your time. I do not want to send a mixed message.

Use both sides of the coin to fill your purse! One side is the intentional, planning, forethought and proactive side. The other is the live in the moment, have fun, surprise each other side. You need both.

I know of a couple who illustrate this. They go on a date each week. They shared how they ended up doing basically the same thing. They went to one of a few places to eat and to the movies. The husband researched and found the top 100 mid-priced restaurants in the metro area they lived. He put the names of the restaurants each on a small slip of paper and put them in a box. Each week, unless one of them really wanted an old favorite, they picked a place from the box and tried it out. The wife looked up community and high school theater groups to go to instead of a movie and surprised him one night with Shakespeare in the Park. The intentional part is the weekly date. The spontaneous part were new activities and restaurants.

Be intentionally spontaneous. Laugh. Go for a walk. Make a new food. Do something fun you haven't ever done before. Enjoy life.

Intentional and Spontaneous Reflection Questions

1. Work is defined as energy expanded to reach a specific goal. Joe said, "It is focused effort and expended energy to reach a desired goal. Your goal is a fulfilling love relationship which illustrates the very love of God to the world. Your goal is creating the happiest place on earth. Your goal is being married to your best friend and enjoying great sex and intimacy. It is a goal worth putting effort into achieving." How much focused effort did you put into these goals last year, based on actual time, energy and money expended? How can you better redirect your energy?

2. Andy Stanley's book, "The Principle of the Path" teaches this truth: Direction determines destination. You can evaluate the direction of your life and extrapolate the destination of it. You can want something, but if you are heading a direction which doesn't lead to that desire, you will not attain it. Based on your direction, what is the destination of your marriage? What do you need to change in your life to begin and travel another direction?

3. Schedule a mini-marriage retreat. It can be one night in a hotel, or better a weekend. The purpose of it is to establish goals. A goal must be a concise sentence stating both a quantifiable outcome and a deadline. Talk about your desired destination in every area of your life, including but not limited to your marriage, finances, spiritual growth, family experiences,

children, personal growth, professional development, etc. Your goals will help you move in the direction you need to reach the destination you desire. Schedule at least two more retreats, one in six months and one in a year to evaluate and change if needed. Marriage takes work: expended energy to reach a desired outcome.

4. Talk to each other about spontaneity in your relationship. Your marriage is not just a cooperative partnership. It is a living and dynamic relationship. When did you last do something completely spontaneous? What are some things you would like to do? Share them with each other. Listen to each other and put it in the back of your mind to just do. If you can do it, do it.

Let's Talk About It

I shared with you my marriage is the best one I have ever heard of. Our marriage is awesome with all capitals. However, it has been 38 years of growth and learning to make it what it is.

I shared how in 1995 God used my wife to reveal to me my heart was not at my home.

In the providence of God, that same day in the mail there was a brochure for a conference called, "Balancing The Pastor's Personal Life" or something like that. It was on the West Coast and specifically targeted good pastors but bad spouses like me. We went. At the conference, three things hit me. The first was the truth God loved me. His love was not conditional or dependent upon my performance. He loved me. Period. End of discussion. The second truth was my life and ministry is a marathon and not a sprint. I treated it like a 100 meter run and not a 26-mile marathon. I needed to stop trying to do everything today. The third thing I learned was the life changing and marriage saving truth that no one on this planet is more important than my wife. Our relationship is to be the primary one. My effectiveness as a father and a pastor hinged upon how good my marriage was.

I committed myself to loving my marriage, not just doing it.

The first thing we realized we had to do was improve our communication. We spent the first fifteen minutes each day talking to each other. We decided on two ground rules. I could not talk about the church or ministry. She could not talk about the children. We wanted to truly talk and communicate, not just report on what was happening in our lives. We explained it to the children. My office was a twenty-minute drive from our house, so I called Denise as I left. She put a cartoon on for the kids and brewed a cup of coffee for the two of us. I arrived home, and we sat on our porch with a nice cup of coffee and looked at each other.

After a few awkward minutes, I said, "I have nothing to say. All I ever talk about is the church. I am embarrassed. I really cannot think of anything."

She answered. "I have nothing either. All I ever talk about are the kids and managing the house."

We stumbled through the first few days with little or no conversation. I bought a book of conversation starters and we used it. It had five levels of open-ended questions and these became our starting points. We moved from struggling to find something to talk about to enjoying our talks. The fifteen minutes became thirty. We disconnected our television and got rid of it. Now instead of staring blankly at a screen, we chatted.

Move forward in time to the present moment. We talk about everything. We talk all the time. She homeschools and I office at home. We eat lunch and dinner together every day. We go out on one lunch date and one dinner date a week. Every afternoon, we walk three to five miles. We spend the entire walk talking to each other. Every night we take a bath together and talk. I tried to keep track of it once and discovered we spent at least three hours a day talking. We talk about theology, current events, plans, goals, ideas, dreams, fears, doubts, emotions, and tasks. We talk and talk and talk. Over three hours a day. How? We still do not have or watch television. We limit time on devices. According to a simple search on the web, the average person spends five hours a day on their device and three hours a day watching television. That means we have eight free hours to spend with each other and our children that you, dear reader, are probably giving to your screens.

If I could point to any one particular skill-set which transformed our marriage, it would probably be communicating. My top two would be instant forgiveness and intentional communication.

Communication is so important God named Himself after it.

No one named God. He named Himself in order to communicate to us His various attributes and character traits. The Trinity chose the name, "Word", for Himself. Jesus, before His incarnation, is/was the Word. Why did He chose this name? Why call Himself the Word? He could have chosen any word or name in the universe. He could have made up His own. He took the word, "Logos" and applied it to Himself. He literally said, "You call me Word. I am the Word." Why this name out of every name in human history? The only explanation is that communication is dear to the heart of God.

Communication is so important God chose to do it and continues to do it.

He gave us His Word, not only in the form of Himself

(Jesus), but in His revelation to us. We could not know Him without His revelation to us. His word reveals Who He is, what He thinks, how He feels, and His desire for us. He revealed Himself to us and then declared His communication to be elevated above His name and to be eternal in nature. Communication is dear to the heart of God.

Communication is so important God wants us to talk to Him constantly.

We are to pray. We are to pray about everything, all the time. We are told to pray without ceasing. Jesus modeled prayer and commanded us to pray. God speaks to us through His Holy Spirit and listens to us in prayer. This is so important the entire Trinity engages with us in prayer. We pray to the Father who listens to us, in the power of the Holy Spirit who leads us, and in the Name of the Son who died for us. Jesus calls Himself our advocate and the Holy Spirit prays for us when we cannot think of what or how to say it. Jesus lives forever to make intercession for us and the Holy Spirit prays for us. They pray to the Father who listens to both of them and to us. God wants us to communicate with Him. Communication is dear to the heart of God.

I challenge couples with this thought. If communication is so important to God that He is the Word, He gave His Word, and through His Word He reveals His character, thoughts, history, plans, and emotions, shouldn't it be important to us in our relationships? God is my example in all of life, therefore I should seek to communicate as He does. Shouldn't I reveal all of these things at bare minimum to my husband or wife?

I am writing an entire book on communication, so in this one I will give and expand upon what I believe is a good definition. When I speak of communication, I am not talking about the shallow, basic, what happened today, type of communication. I refer to deep and serious discussions. Denise and I apply this to our children, especially our adult ones. We also use it in counseling and in normal friendships.

Communication is the process of revealing to someone what I think and how I feel in such a manner that understanding and empathy occur.

I put this working definition together based on how God communicates to us. Revelation was and is a process. He did not word dump Genesis 1:1 through Revelation 22:21. It was a process over a long period of time. He revealed it to someone. He did not just reveal it to the author who wrote it down. He revealed and reveals it to us as He speaks thorough the Holy Spirit illuminating and explaining His Word. Since He revealed it to us, He did it in our language in order for us to understand it. He entered into our world, both in the written Word and the incarnation of Christ.

His Word reveals His thoughts and plans for us. I can know God's will for my life, and God's perspective on life, because He revealed it to me.

I also know how He feels. I see His emotions in and through the Word. He did all of this in a manner which allows me to understand and empathize. His goal in communication was not speaking. His goal is/was for me to hear and understand.

This is how we should approach communication in our relationships. We seek to enter into their world and allow them to be understood and to understand. Communication doesn't happen unless both the speaker and the listener connect. I can talk all day long. I do not even need someone to be there. I can talk to myself. Communication involves at the bare minimum two focused people.

Let's look at this definition again and break it down in our marriage.

Communication is the process of revealing to someone what I think and how I feel in such a manner that understanding and empathy occur.

The first part is to understand the idea of communicating. I am not talking. I am not giving my defense. I am not arguing or proving my point. The purpose of deep communication is not to win. It is to understand and be understood. I want to enter into your world and have you be a part of mine.

Communication is a process.

A great example is found in the story of our relationship above. Denise and I could not fill up a 15 minutes time period. We started at zero. It is like learning math. We had to learn to count before we could move on to calculus. It is a process. Sometimes the process focuses on a particular topic or subject. Denise and I have shared a lot through the years about our lives and childhood and how it impacts us today. We examined presuppositions and ideas about parenting, discipline and in-laws. The topic of parenting and discipline has been in process for over thirty years as we continue to grow. It is also communication itself that is a process. We began at zero and now we talk over three hours every day.

Communication is a process of revealing to someone.

The process is connected to the revelation. I reveal myself to you. This is vital in a friendship and a marriage. The longer we are married, the less communicating and the more assuming we do. We just think we know how the other person feels or what they think. We operate out of our, more often than not, erroneous assumptions. The truth is the Bible teaches it is impossible for us to know what is in the heart or mind of someone else. Only God can see inside. The only way, I will say it again for emphasis, the only way someone can know what I think is for me to reveal it to them. The only way someone else can know how I feel is for me to reveal it to them. Denise and I have been married since 1984 and communicate more than any couple I know. Yet, I still do not know what she thinks or feels unless she tells me. It is a lifelong process because we grow and change. I am not the same man that Denise married. I have changed my opinions and perspectives on so many things. I am not as hard as I was. I am not as opinionated. I am not as arrogant. I am far more in touch with my emotions. I understand the complexity of the personality God has given me. I have been hurt and hurt others. All of these things change me. I have to not only examine myself in order to understand myself, I need to reveal to her what I discover about what is going on inside of me. It is a process.

Communication is the process of revealing to someone what I think.

I mentioned before one of the dangers of long-term relationships is assuming I know the inner workings of the other person. I think I know what they think. I then respond or react to what I think they think. They do the same thing. It ends up like being a copy of a copy of a copy. It is like the game of telephone where the final message is nothing like the original statement. My reaction to her reaction, to my reaction, to her reaction, to what she thought, I thought she thought…Do you see the problem?

The truth is, no one other than God knows our thoughts. God can see our thoughts and knows them. He is the only One. Even the devil cannot read our minds. Therefore, the only way my wife (husband) can know what I think is for me to reveal it to them through communication. One thing I have discovered is many times the only way I can truly know my own thoughts is to seek to put them into words. As I formulate sentences to explain or describe my thoughts, I begin to understand them for myself. I uncover my own mind. This is the point of the word 'reveal'. It is a process in which I reveal, uncover, open, expose, disclose, and bring out into the open the thoughts hidden inside of me. I form words to paint a picture of who I am to someone else.

Communication is the process of revealing to someone what I think and how I feel.

This is vital, and one aspect of intimate communication, I have discovered most men find more difficult than women. In the same manner which another person can assume or attempt to guess what someone is thinking; we can only guess what someone is feeling unless they tell us. I never knew how far off I was from knowing Denise's emotions until we started practicing a communication model. When we are having a truly serious discussion, we will listen to the other person without interruption or comment. Once they finish their speaking, we respond by restating their words and emotions in our own language. "If I understand you, this is what you said. This is what you think and, based upon it, this is how you feel. You feel like…" When we first started doing this, I would easily paraphrase what Denise said. That is a no brainier. Then, when I tried to reverse engineer from what she said to what she thought, to restate it in my own language going to root ideas and motives, I would often miss. The last stage of explaining how this made her feel was a continual failure. I simply did not connect with her emotions. I thought I did. I assumed. Through the process of trying to restate her emotions with my own words, I realized I was emotionally ignorant. To me, a great example is the color palette. I operated with five or six basic emotional colors such as happy, sad, or mad. Maybe I could throw in another one periodically, but I pretty much stayed in these lanes. I discovered Denise is more like a 4K computer screen with 512 million emotional color options. My five basic colors could not paint the vibrant picture of Denise's heart. Over time, I expanded my own emotional palette. It happened as she revealed herself to me. No one can know what you think, or how you feel, unless you choose to reveal it.

Communication is the process of revealing to someone what I think and how I feel in such a manner that understanding occurs.

The last part of my definition focuses on what I perceive to be the ignored part of communication. In public speaking, there are four distinct aspects to consider. The speaker is the easiest since it is me. The content is the second part. I need to know what I am going to say. The third is the medium or method of communicating it. Pastors focus on the second and give a little thought to the third, and that is the summation of their preparation. That is why many sermons or lessons are boring. We believe vomiting out information is communication.

More than once, I have heard or read pastors who say, "My job is to teach the truth. What they do with it is up to them." This is accurate to a point. It is our job to teach the truth. I expand on this. "It is my job to teach the truth in a manner which allows them to easily understand the truth and its implications for their lives. I am to teach in their language, with illustrations from their daily lives, using descriptive phrases and words they use and understand." This is what God did for us. He came into our world and communicated to us in our language and context.

Go back to the components of communication. The speaker and the content are not the only aspects, nor are they the focus. The third one, how I communicate, is just as important as what I say. If I preach a great evangelical sermon and thoroughly explain the gospel, it will do nothing if I don't do it in the language of the listener. If I preach in Spanish to a Chinese-speaking crowd, did I really preach the gospel? If the listener cannot understand the speaker, is it communication?

The final aspect is the listener. I need to focus on them. In the famous book, Seven Habits of Highly Effective People, Stephen Covey coins a phrase I use constantly. "Seek first to understand, then be understood." If I am to communicate with my audience, I must understand them. In my pastor conferences, I use the example of telling the story of David and Goliath. If I am teaching this story to a group of four-year-olds, I concentrate on the simple truth of God not being limited in His ability to use us. I act the story out with armies on both sides of the room and I scream out Goliath's part.

In church, I have a ten-year-old come stand at the foot of the stage and I tower a good four feet above him to illustrate the size variance. I point out David was probably 9 or 10.

To the pastors, I show them David's age as we see he had eight older brothers, but only two of them were serving in the army, therefore over 20. He had six brothers under 20 but older than him and none of them were twins. I then point out the theological cycles of the passage in relation to others and give the pastors two or three sermon ideas of application. In every situation, the speaker and the content were the same. I told the story of David and Goliath. The third aspect, how I told it and what I focused upon, was contingent and dependent upon the fourth part, the listener.

This is true in public and private communication. I must reveal to my wife what I am thinking in her language, verbal and non-verbal. I do not simply reveal my thoughts. I do it in a manner which allows understanding to happen. I think about how I say what I say. My goal is not to reveal my thoughts. My ultimate goal is for her to understand both what I think and why I think it. I need to concentrate on helping her understand. How can I explain myself to her in a manner which promotes her understanding me?

Communication is the process of revealing to someone what I think and how I feel in such a manner that understanding and empathy occur.

The same truth applies to revealing my feelings. I do not want to just tell her how I feel. I want her to empathize with me. I want to bring her into my heart so she feels what I feel. The word compassion is an illustration of this. It literally means with the same feeling. I do not want her to know I am sad. I want her to understand where my sadness originated and how deep it is. To accomplish this, I need to express my feelings in her language. Once more, God is our example. He uses our words and emotions to reveal His emotions and feelings to us. He entered into our emotional world.

Communication is the process of revealing to someone what I think and how I feel in such a manner that understanding and empathy occur.

This is the heart of a deep and intimate relationship. Our relationship will go no deeper than my revelation of my inner self takes it.

Let's Talk About It Reflection Questions

1. Joe said something profound happened after he understood God's love. He said, "I committed myself to loving my marriage, not just doing it." Do you love your marriage? Justify your response.

2. Joe said that after over thirty years of marriage counseling and almost forty of being married, the number one skill to develop in a relationship is how to communicate. Discuss this in light of God's communication to us. He named Himself the Word. He gave us His Word. He speaks to us through the Holy Spirit and His Word. He elevated His Word above His Name. His Word is eternal. If communication is this important to God, how important is it, and should it be, to me?

3. Commit to communication and follow the same pattern Joe and Denise followed. Agree to talk 15-30 minutes each day, but you cannot talk about your jobs or your children.

4. Go over each part of the communication definition and evaluate yourself and your marriage: Communication is the process of revealing to someone what I think and how I feel in such a manner that understanding and empathy occur.

Get Your Conflict On

Best friendships somehow can survive conflict. Friends can disagree and still be friends. I share often the truth I already shared in previous chapters. Denise and I never argue or fight. We simply do not. I spoke on this at a family conference and did something spontaneous. Six of my adult children lived close enough to the conference to attend it. Without warning, I called them up to the stage and had them sit as if they were a panel.

"My children are here and I want to do something unplanned as an illustration. Instead of me telling you about our marriage and home, I will let them." I said. I looked at them and admonished them to tell the honest and open truth. I then asked.

"Share with everyone the subject of the last argument you heard, or know, mom and I had."

No one could think of an example. My daughter Faith, who was married with two kids, said, "I cannot ever remember you and mom having an argument."

My son Ben, 25, said, "We never heard or saw you argue, but more than that. I do not know of a single time you had an argument." The other kids said basically the same thing.

"What about just overall attitude or conduct? How did we handle problems.?" I asked. They all said the same basic thing. They did not know of us to have a disagreement or problem.

My daughter Hope, 20, said, "You guys talked all the time and we would hear you discuss options. It was like you parented us. I cannot remember you ever raising your voice or being visually or verbally angry. You would discuss the event and then bring consequences to bear. I would hear you and mom talking about something and a lot of times you would both express different opinions or viewpoints. However, it was always calm and kind. I know you disagreed, but you did not do it in a mean way."

The panel continued for a few minutes. It was a wonderful illustration of the truth that we can have conflict without sin.

We live in a world of conflict. I think the aspect of American culture that stands out the most to someone who has lived in another country for over a decade is our conflict. Our only actual connection with American culture for almost 20 years has been social media. It is ugly. People are just mean to each other. If you follow me on any (anti)social media platform, you have seen me post myriads of times admonitions to Christians about hateful speech, gossip, backbiting, whispering, complaining, and just being mean. All those verses that apply to speech apply to written words as well. It looks like America could be summed up with the word 'conflict'. In the lesson I referred to and used the panel in, I pointed out how we have conflict in our workplaces, churches, families, and homes. You can do an internet search for yourself and you will discover conflict, divisiveness and arguing are the norm.

We live in a world of conflict. We are a house divided on a national and personal level. We argue and fight over almost everything. In my opinion, the most damaging thing of the whole CoVid experience in 2020-2021 was the manner in which we responded to people who disagreed with our opinions. The only word to sum it up is this: Hate.

Yet in reality, the normal thing to do is to disagree and love, disagree and live, disagree and have it strengthen your relationship.

Conflict is normal. Conflict is not the problem. In our marriage, Denise and I have conflict almost every day. Our kids could not think of examples of us fighting or arguing because we resolve our conflict in the early stages. We have conflict. We disagree. We disagree on memories and plans. I cannot count how many times one of us told a story only to have the other one correct details of the story, such as the characters in it, the location, or the time. We will disagree on which child or who said what. It is a conflict.

Conflict is normal. Conflict happens whenever two wills differ. When we are in the States it is all about the food. We maximize our time to get a taste of home from places we miss. We went on a date. I informed Denise we were going to Red Robin to get a hamburger. She disagreed and wanted to go to On The Border and have enchiladas. It was a rare moment, because neither one of us wanted to back down. I wanted a burger. She wanted enchiladas. It was a conflict.

I desire one thing and she wants something different. We have a conflict. The presence of multiple choices and multiple free wills brings conflict. Jesus prayed three different times for the cup of the Father's wrath, the cross, to be taken from Him. Jesus, in His humanity, did not want to suffer and die. Yet, He resolved the conflict by joyfully submitting to the will of the Father. "Now what I will, but what you will."

It is not the presence of conflict which is the issue. It is what the conflict tempts us to do and how we respond to the temptation. Our response to the conflict is the issue. When my will collides with Denise's will and conflict sparks, we are both tempted to respond to the conflict in a sinful manner, fanning the spark of conflict into a relationship consuming fire. My flesh tempted me to argue, manipulate, and push for my burger. I really wanted one. So far, in our conflict, no sin occurred, but it was about to. She wanted an enchilada, and I wanted a burger. You might laugh as you read this, but what do you usually experience conflict, argue and fight about? How often is it really something trivial and simple? How often does a hamburger date hurt your marriage?

The key is to respond to the conflict in a way that honors Christ, builds the relationship, and solves problems. How do you do this? How can I testify our marriage of almost forty years is argument and fight-free? How can our children say they grew up in a home where people did not lose their temper or express their viewpoints sinfully? How do you manage interpersonal conflict in your marriage and home? Go back to the one-another list. Denise is the hero here. She said, "Let's go get a burger tonight. On The Border isn't going anywhere, and we can grab enchiladas some other time. I see you really want one."

The first thing is always the first thing. We are to do everything to the glory of God.

"Therefore, whether you eat or drink, or whatever you do, do all things for the glory of God." (1 Corinthians 10.31)

This includes how we respond to conflict.

The way we think of our spouse, their motives, opinions or plans must bring glory to God. When our wills collide, the very first thing to do is to stop and bring your thoughts captive into obedience to Jesus.

Think about what typically happens. There is a conflict. It is a little thing such as burger or enchilada. Then, in our mind, this little thing begins to grow. "Why do I always give in? Why does she always pick the place we eat? She is my wife, not my mom. She pushes and pushes and pushes. She did this last night with the movie. I did not want to watch that stupid movie. She did. Yesterday I wanted to write, but she made me go to Walmart because she did not want to go alone. Push push push. It is always…"

Now it is no longer about a burger. Satan has taken a little lie and made it a bonfire. You are angry and it is not because you want medium rare meat with fries. You ascribe poor motivation. You make mental accusations. You remember wrongs and distort them towards your victimization. Now, it is not the burger! You must fight for manhood itself!

This is why we argue over trivial things.

95% of the time someone comes into my office for marriage counseling, the reason they are there is not the reason they are there. When they voice their problems to me, even to them, it sounds so trite and trivial.

What God teaches us to do is examine our thoughts. If they do not line up with the mind of Christ, we repent of them and replace them. I must think about what God thinks about this situation. If the conflict tempts me to think negatively about my husband or wife, I must respond to the temptation with truth and think of them with Jesus' thoughts. Instead of listening to the lies of satan and my own flesh about my spouse, I need to recite and focus on who God says she is.

My attitude must bring glory to God. A thought is a quick idea, word, or judgement which pops into my mind. My attitude results from dwelling on these thoughts. It is an overall disposition. In our conflict, my attitude should be one of self-less serving and humility. The attitude which was in Christ was to humble Himself and serve. This should be my attitude. Most of our sinful responses to conflict arise from selfishness. In hindsight, I selfishly wanted the burger bad enough to upset my wife. It became more and more the food of my dreams. I really wanted it. My selfish heart tempted me to impose my desire over hers. I will want to force the issue and manipulate things in order to get my bacon burger. She responded to God's glory. Her self-less service and joyful submission reminded her this is not the only time she will ever have an opportunity to eat. She served me. I can joyfully wolf down a burger now, and she knows her enchiladas are coming soon. She realized a burger would make me happy, so if something that little can bring me joy, then she would buy a burger. Her thoughts brought glory to God.

My words must bring glory to God. I discussed the importance of both what we say and how we say it in the previous chapter. If I feel the need or desire to continue in the conflict in order to get the outcome I prefer, I need to choose my words carefully. It thrilled my heart when Hope said, "I would hear you and mom talking about something and a lot of times you would both express different opinions or viewpoints. However, it was always calm and kind. I know you disagreed, but you did not do it in a mean way." In the great burger/enchilada battle which lasted three minutes, we never spoke with harsh words or tone. This is the point. I can express my thoughts and feelings, my desires, memories, and ideas in an unoffensive and gracious manner. I can disagree without being a jerk or meanie. I need to remember I am called and enabled by my Savior to speak graciously. Evil speech is put off from me and now it is kindness who guides my responses. Our thoughts bring glory to God and those thoughts make it to our mouth. Out of the abundance of the heart, the mouth speaks.

My actions must glorify my Savior. They will if my thoughts, attitudes, and words precede them. What I do when I face conflict needs to point to my love and worship of God. I must do what brings Him the most glory. God is seeking glory through how I respond to good and bad. I am His holy instrument and am to be used by Him. I can not be an instrument in His hands if I am not clean, if I sully myself with sinful actions. Not only do my thoughts, attitudes, and words need to bring glory to the One Who died for me, my actions do too.

Consider simply applying this one principle to your marriage. What if, whenever you experienced a conflict, you sought to glorify the Father with your thoughts, attitudes, words, and actions? What if your foremost goal was not to win the conflict and get your way, but to allow God to receive honor from your responses to the conflict? How much would it improve your marriage? How much would it improve all of your relationships? It only takes one person. Denise did it and we loved our burger date. A few nights later, we loved our enchiladas as well. Both times, we loved each other and Jesus.

Denise and I started seeking to apply this one over-arching principle to our marriage within the first couple of years. We stated it out loud. We told each other. "I want to always respond to you and to our circumstances in a Christ honoring and God glorifying manner." This focus can stop so much sin and defeat so many temptations.

The second key to managing interpersonal conflict and resolving it quickly and satisfactorily is to examine the fruit revealed by the conflict. God focuses on fruit. I invested at least one chapter on our fruit in both of my books, "Before You Go" and "Discipleship of the Heart". I recommend you get them and read them. God wants us to look inside before we look outside. Our fruit is the knee-jerk reaction the event tempts us to take. We may not do it, but the fact we wanted to do it shows us our heart. If my initial reaction to the circumstances or conflict is not one of love, joy, peace, gentleness, etc., then I can see my need for Christ. Before I address the conflict or my spouse, I must go to Calvary and have my heart cleansed. God used this moment to show me why Jesus died for me. Jesus died for me because I am the type of person who would be angry at my wife for not wanting a hamburger. I need Jesus. We have a saying in our family, "Por eso Jesus murió", or "This is why Jesus died." To us it means Jesus came and died because without His forgiveness and His Spirit living in me, I am controlled by my own foolish desires and put myself above all else. It reminds me that I need to go to the cross and repent once again for being that sort of man.

Conflict reveals my heart and my need for Jesus. This is why Jesus died. He died because I am such a sinner that I would be tempted to use harsh words and hurt my wife simply because she thought a detail in my story was not totally accurate. My fruit, my initial knee-jerk reaction, reveals my thoughts and attitude. If it is not the fruit of the Holy Spirit, then I have something more important than where to eat that I must deal with. I have a sinful heart which needs to be washed whiter than snow.

The third key to peacefully resolving conflict is humility. This goes along with serving the other person, but deals more with heart than action. Service is an action. Humility is a disposition. A great example is in story details. How many times have you either done this or seen this done? Someone tells a story. They say something like, "Once, about 10 years ago, me and my friend Bobby...." The spouse listening interrupts and corrects a detail. Something like, "It was only six years ago." Or, "It wasn't Bobby. He was not there. It was Sam." The person telling the story disagrees and they talk, then become agitated, then maybe end up in a full-fledged argument, which spans time and is brought up again at a later fight. The truth is, the date of the event or the particular friend who was there were not important to the point of the story being made.

Humility would do this. I teach it to my kids. "Whenever we have a disagreement, it is because two people think they are right. One, or both, of the people is/are wrong, but they believe they are right. They are wrong, but they are convinced it is the other person who is wrong. One person is wrong, no matter how much they feel they are right. No one would ever be wrong by definition if they knew they were wrong. What makes them wrong is they think they are right. Now, what I need to remember is that person, the wrong one, could be me just as easily as it could be them. I can think I am right and still be wrong. My thinking I am right does not make me right. Nor does my thinking they are wrong make them wrong."

Humility reminds me of my humanity. Go back to the story.

"Once, about 10 years ago…"

"It wasn't that long ago. It was more like six years ago. Remember, our daughter was there, and she was not fifteen yet…"

"I thought it was longer than that, but I could be wrong. Many times I get dates wrong. So, once, not many years ago, I was with my friend and…"

Conflict and conflict resolved. I thought it was ten years. She thought it was six. One of us is wrong. As I told the story, I thought it was Denise. I felt like she corrected a detail and it did not need to be corrected. I was right about the timeline. I also knew it did not matter. Plus, my continual thinking I was right doesn't mean she is wrong. It could be me. It did not matter. Why have a major fight over a minor detail? If the hill is not worth dying on, why fight over it? End of the story is, on the way home we talked about something else and in the middle of our conversation I realized she was correct. It was six years. ;)

Another key to easily resolving conflict goes back to communication. Seek first to understand and then to be understood. Do not argue over something if you do not know for sure what you are fighting for or against. If you and your spouse have a disagreement or conflict, then start seeking to understand them. Try to find out what they think, why they think it, how they feel and why they feel that way.

Instead of bulldozing them over to get your will done, seek to fully understand their will.

Let me share a bigger example to illustrate my point. I am writing this during a critical time in our country concerning racism. Our culture is seeking to resolve racism, or seeking to show there is no racism to resolve. I am a white man. I am a white man who grew up in the South. I am a white man who grew up in the South in Mansfield, Texas. You can google Mansfield and segregation to get insight into this. I am a white man who grew up in the South in Mansfield, Texas, raised in a racist family. All of these combined in my life to make my default setting one that denied racism and dismissed any evidence of it. By default, I wanted to discredit those who spoke of its continued existence because of who I was. It was not because I studied the evidence and concluded through it they were wrong. It is because of my default setting. The environment in which I had been brought up had programmed me. Default settings are easy because they require no change.

But after becoming a Christian, I decided to listen to the majority voice of non-white people in America. Instead of attacking their viewpoint and defending mine, I asked myself if they could give me insight I do not possess. I read books which disagreed with my default setting. I watched documentaries presenting another side. I educated myself. But most importantly, I developed friendships with African Americans and other minorities. It is way easier to be against an idea if that idea doesn't have a body with thoughts, emotions, and experiences. It's easier to be against an idea, than a friend. I cannot evaluate a position on a socio-economical, or political opinion if I do not examine it, and often the best way to examine it is to become friends with those on the opposing side and then to have open, honest discussions with them. The purpose is to understand what a different side thinks and feels and why they think it. To see from their perspective. What kind of missionaries would we be if we discounted the opinions and experiences of the people of Bolivia or Ghana simply because they were not our experiences and our initial, uninformed opinion differed?

My default setting was wrong because of the environment in which I had been raised, and I hadn't before sought to understand an opposing side. I now more fully understand the real, not the demonized version, the honest viewpoint of my African American and minority friends. Through seeking to understand another viewpoint, I actually discovered I was the one who had been wrong. So, I began to reprogram my default setting.

I believe you cannot really participate in honest dialogue unless you can graciously, calmly, and accurately state what the opposing side thinks. It does not mean you agree or disagree with them. It means you understand them.

This is true on a macro and micro level. When we have conflict, we need to listen to the other viewpoint with a desire to understand their reason and emotions. Not to argue or to discredit, but to enter into their world. I want to know their viewpoint and not just defend mine. The goal is not to prove I am right. It is to resolve the conflict for the glory of God. Always put the relationship above the win and remember WE are greater than ME. Some things are worth fighting for, but most of our fights are not for those things.

Best friends experience conflict. So do even the best marriages. Conflict is not sin. It is a temptation to sin. Best friends resolve the conflict.

Get Your Conflict On Reflection Questions

1. Joe said, "It is not the presence of conflict which is the issue. It is what the conflict tempts us to do and how we respond to the temptation. Our response to the conflict is the issue." Do you agree or disagree and why?

2. Consider simply applying this one principle to your marriage. What if, whenever you experienced a conflict, you sought to glorify the Father with your thoughts, attitudes, words and actions? What if your foremost goal was not to win the conflict and get your way, but rather to allow God to receive honor from your responses to the conflict? How much would it improve your marriage? How much would it improve all of your relationships?

3. What would happen if you applied the one-anothers from the earlier chapter to the event?

4. What fruit do you typically see in your life from conflict?

5. Joe said,"God wants us to look inside before we look outside." How can God use conflict to help you become more like Jesus?

6. Another principle to manage conflict is humility. Humility reminds me of my humanity. Someone is wrong and it could be me. Don't have a major battle on a minor hill. Do you typically have conflict over

little and perhaps irrelevant things? How can humility help stop it?

7. The Bible says an understanding person has patience. Seek first to understand and then be understood is the principle. Is your goal in conflict to understand and empathize or win?

a. Discuss this: Our fruit is the knee-jerk reaction the event tempts us to take. We may not do it, but the fact we wanted to do it reveals to us our heart. If my initial reaction to the circumstances or conflict is not one of love, joy, peace, gentleness, etc., then I can see my need for Christ. Before I address the conflict or my spouse, I must go to Calvary and have my heart cleansed. God used this moment to show me why Jesus died for me.

b. "Whenever we have a disagreement, it is because two people think they are right. One, or both, of the people are wrong but they really believe they are right. They are wrong, but they are convinced it is the other person who is wrong. One person is wrong no matter how much they feel they are right. What I need to remember is that person, the wrong one, could be me just as easily as it could be them. I can think I am right and still be wrong. My thinking I am right does not make me right. Nor does my thinking they are wrong make them wrong." Discuss this. Do you ever truly believe it might be YOU who is wrong? Why not?

Instant And Complete Forgiveness

There are very few things which I would label essential to life and/or solid relationships. In the chapter on communication, I already revealed them. Intentional communication and instant forgiveness are the labels which I give to them. We must communicate all the time and we must forgive, and I mean this, all the time.

Denise is in the States as I type this sentence. There was a death in the family so she went to be with her parents in Texas. While there, my daughter in Florida went into early labor so Denise jumped on a plane to go be with her. At the same time, my mother-in-law needed a cataract surgery the day after my father-in-law had an in-patient medical procedure performed. There is a five-hour time difference between us at the moment. I called her to talk, and accidentally called too early. These events, as well as jet lag, and being on a different continent combined to tempt Denise to speak harshly to me. God grace allowed me to respond in a loving and kind manner.

Less than five minutes after our conversation, the phone rang. Denise called me back. "Honey, I am sorry. I spoke harshly to you and I should not have. I sinned. Will you please forgive me?"

I assured her it was done. I forgave her before the phones disconnected the first time. She did not need to ask. It was already given.

If there is any one thing to sum up our entire Christian faith, it is forgiveness. Christianity revolves around the hub of forgiveness. The foundation of our faith is forgiveness. It is our purpose. The symbol of our faith is the cross. Jesus died on the cross to grant us forgiveness. Our message is we can have our sins forgiven. It is the life, death and resurrection of Jesus can forgive us of all our sins if we will repent and ask Him. God calls us to be forgiven and to forgive.

Forgiveness is not an option.

Forgiveness is not earned.

Forgiveness is a gift given to the receiver the moment it is needed.

We live in a fallen world. Hurt people who hurt people surround us. The world is full of people who are sinners and whose sins hurt others.

Our parents are sinners.

Our siblings are sinners.

Our church members are sinners.

Our friends are sinners.

Our classmates are sinners.

Our workmates are sinners.

Our spouses are sinners.

We are sinners.

So why does it surprise us when people sin?

All of us have two things in common. We are sinners and we sin. The result of those two things is often our interactions hurt others. The truth is, the sinful actions and attitudes of others hurt us.

I once heard that the summary of a Christian marriage is this: A Christian marriage is made up by two forgiven sinners who forgive sinners. I expand that in my teaching and use it to describe the Christian life. A forgiven person who forgives people. It is that simple.

There is an incredible truth we need to comprehend. Before we came to Christ, we sinned because we are sinners. After coming to Christ, we are no longer sinners by nature. We now are redeemed and forgiven. We have been reborn. Transformed. Remade. The truth is sinners respond sinfully to sin. We are not sinners. We do not have to respond sinfully to sin. As children of God, we can choose to respond in a Christlike manner to bring glory to God when folks sin against us. We are not forgiven sinners. We are forgiven Christians. Our identity is not in who we were before Christ forgave us. It is who we are afterwards. I am a forgiven person called to forgive people.

Denise did not marry a sinner. She married a saint who sins. I am a child of God. I am not perfect and I do sin, but the core of my identity is in Jesus. I do not have to sin. I do not have to respond sinfully to sin. I can respond holy to sin. He redeemed me and empowered me to do just that.

If we are going to be like Jesus, we must forgive like Him.

Not forgiving is a sin. I do not have the option of forgiving or not forgiving. I must forgive. Many times in my counseling ministry, I have had to deal with this truth. A couple will come to me because of some sin which one committed and, without knowing it, because of the sin of unforgiveness being committed. I had a couple come because the wife committed the sin of adultery. This sin is not what ultimately destroyed their marriage. Her sin tempted her husband to commit the sin of unforgiveness. He refused to forgive her. Her sin was a huge, onetime event she confessed and repented of. His continual and unrepentant sin of bitterness destroyed what was left of their relationship.

If you are a follower of Christ, then you must forgive those who wrong you. There is no option.

Be kind to one another, tender-hearted, forgiving each other, just as God in Christ also has forgiven you. (Ephesians 4:32)

So, as those who have been chosen of God, holy and beloved, put on a heart of compassion, kindness, humility, gentleness and patience; bearing with one another, and forgiving each other, whoever has a complaint against anyone; just as the Lord forgave you, so also should you. (Colossians 3:12-13)

Love is patient, love is kind and is not jealous; love does not brag and is not arrogant, does not act unbecomingly; it does not seek its own, is not provoked, does not take into account a wrong suffered, (1 Corinthians 13:4-5)

Above all, keep fervent in your love for one another, because love covers a multitude of sins. (1 Peter 4:8)

For if you forgive others for their transgressions, your heavenly Father will also forgive you. But if you do not forgive others, then your Father will not forgive your transgressions. (Matthew 6:14-15)

See to it that no one comes short of the grace of God; that no root of bitterness springing up causes trouble, and by it many be defiled; (Hebrews 12:15)

I believe the lack of forgiveness is the root cause of almost every divorce. Seldom does a marriage end, or become lifeless and only on paper, because of some huge event. We even have a word for it. We call it irreconcilable differences. Marriages have major crises. However, in my experience, it isn't a large problem which ends the relationship. It is how we respond to the large and small problems. We do not forgive each other. The lack of gratefulness, unkind words, small irritations, little snips, and being neglected add up when not forgiven. It isn't a snotty remark which leads to a broken relationship. It is the unforgiven stockpile of other things. The remark is the final straw.

I illustrated this in my church with a volunteer. I had a young married man come on the stage.

"I want to show you how not forgiving others affects your life."

I pick up a chair. "This is something your wife did to you. She was disrespectful or did not meet your expectations, or something like that. It could actually be something you thought she did, but in reality, she did nothing. You thought she thought something. Whatever it is, it is a wrong suffered." I put the chair in his arms.

I pick up another one and repeat the process two times. I label the chairs with various possible minor offenses in their marriage. I then move on. I pick up the music stand on the stage. "This is a wrong done to you by a coworker. They took credit for a joint project or gossiped about you. They hurt you in some way."

I move on to a few more objects until their arms are full.

"Now, I know you love Jesus and the church. I need some help. Can you help me move the pulpit to over there?" He stands and looks perplexed. He starts to put the chairs and other objects down to help. "No. You must continue to carry those burdens. Grab the other side." He cannot.

I call his little three-year-old on the stage and pick her up. "Your daughter loves you and needs you. Here, give her a hug."

He cannot reach her or hug her.

"I want all of you to notice something. His life is full of wrongs. People from his family, work, friends and past have all hurt him. However, not one of these things in his arms is from me or the church. I did not sin against him or hurt him. Yet, he will not help me. He can't. Too many burdens weigh him down. Look at his precious daughter. She did not put a single item in his arms, but she suffers from them. He cannot be the father she needs him to be because his father hurt him and he still carries the hurt."

I turn to him. "Will you forgive your father?"

"Yes."

I take the item I placed in his arms as a sin from his father off.

"Will you forgive your co-worker for this?" I point to the chair labeled gossip.

"Yes."

This process continues until his arms are empty.

"Can you hug your daughter and carry her back to her seat?"

He picks her up, and she kisses him spontaneously. It is perfect.

"When we refuse to forgive, it impacts the whole of our life. Also, notice this. Every burden, offense, and wrong he carried were not in the arms of the person who hurt him. His father isn't even alive. We do not hurt those who hurt us by not forgiving them. We perpetuate the hurt caused and the enemy of our soul uses it to cause hurt to others. He could not serve his church, meet the needs of his child, or do anything to help his wife because of all the hurt he still carried. Once he forgave, it freed him. Go back to his father. It did not free his father. His dad has been in heaven for several years. It freed him. Not forgiving others hurts us and those around us. Forgiving others frees us and those around us."

This is truth. In your marriage, if you do not forgive, it compounds the next infraction and makes it more difficult for you to do the right thing. I have seen people who cannot maintain any relationship now because of the hurt they received decades ago. Forgiveness is so vital to life that I made it one of the last words I ever spoke to my 29-year-old son before he went to heaven. He was in the ICU and everyone knew without a divine miracle he was minutes from leaving this world. I leaned over and whispered into his ear. I said several things, but this was one of them. "Son, I want you to know I forgive you. If there is anything in your life where you feel like you have hurt me, I forgive you. If you think you wronged me, I forgive you. If in any way whatsoever you think I am offended or let down by you, I forgive you. Also, if I have hurt or wronged you, please forgive me. If I did something I should not have, or did not do something I should have, please forgive me. Step into eternity, forgiven and forgiving." Whenever I hold a funeral service, I take a few moments of the message to tell those present to forgive any wrongs committed by the deceased. Forgiveness frees us, and lack of forgiveness places us in bondage. So, how do we forgive?

The best way to be an instant forgiver is to constantly go before God to be forgiven. We need forgiveness. One of the greatest marks of Christian maturity is understanding our past forgiveness and our present need. We need Jesus. The more I live in the presence of His forgiveness and seek it instantly as I sin, the easier it is to instantly forgive others.

"And forgive us our sins, just as we have forgiven those who have sinned against us." Matthew 6:12

The first thing to do is to go back to the basics. God forgave you. He forgave you, if you have given your life to Jesus Christ, for every sin you committed before salvation and every sin you will commit in the future. He forgave past, present, and future sin on the cross. You are forgiven. I said earlier a Christian marriage comprises two forgiven people. Let God's forgiveness for the depth of your sin penetrate your soul. You are forgiven. It is out of that forgiveness that you have the power to forgive. You can forgive others because God has forgiven you! It is like a bank account. If I deposit $1,000,000 in my account every morning, then I can afford to write a $1 check once a day. When you realize God has deposited infinite forgiveness to us, we can give it to someone else.

The second thing to do is think in terms of instantaneous

forgiveness. I use a phrase an elder in my church, Bill Parker, taught me decades ago. The phrase is: Short Sin Account. The idea is the moment we realize we sinned; we run to the cross and ask for forgiveness. We do not wait. The Holy Spirit shows a sin to you. You, the moment you see it, ask for forgiveness in Christ. Be instantaneous in your asking for forgiveness. With that same idea in mind, give forgiveness instantaneously. In my family, we use the phrase, "instant forgiveness". The moment you are sinned against, hurt, wronged, or whatever phrase you used to describe it, in that moment, give forgiveness. Do not wait until they know they sinned. Do not wait for them to confess or ask for forgiveness. Forgive them instantly the moment you realize they wronged you. If, not when, but if they realize their sin and ask you to forgive them, you can easily do it because it is already done. In the phone's example call I presented earlier, I forgave Denise. We spoke, and she was unkind. When we hung up, I, out loud, prayed for her and expressed to God my forgiveness of her. When she called to ask, it was already done. She might have lived another fifty years and never even remember or think she did anything wrong. I still forgave.

"And don't sin by letting anger gain control over you. Don't let the sun go down while you are still angry." Ephesians 4:26

When we first got married, I would get up and eat a bowl of cereal for breakfast. Then I would put the leftover cereal and bowl by the sink. Denise came to me and asked me to please rinse the bowl out as soon as I finished the cereal. She pointed out that when I rinsed it immediately, all it took was a little water. But when I would leave it, the cereal would form an unbreakable bond with the bowl. It would take scrubbing to get the milk scum and cereal out.

That is how it is with forgiveness. If you do it immediately, right off, just rinse it out and be done with it…then it is over and you are ready to go on with a clean conscience and heart. But if you wait, it hardens, clings to your soul, and it takes more intensive effort to get it out. The best way to forgive is before you have time to harden!

Once you forgive, choose to not think about the offense. It will sometimes enter your thoughts unbidden. It just walks into the room of your thoughts. You can't help that, but you do not need to offer it a chair to sit down and stay a while. When you think about the offense, choose to remember and remind yourself of the forgiveness granted by you to them and to you by Christ. On a regular basis, I will need to find a file on my computer. I will search for it and occasionally click on the wrong folder or file. As soon as it opens, I realize what I have done. Guess what I do? I close the file. I am not trapped. I do not have to work on the open file. I am not forced to read it. I see it is wrong and I close it. This is how forgiveness works. Something triggers the memory of a past and forgiven event. I immediately choose to remember the forgiveness and then think about something else. It really is that simple.

Instant And Complete Forgiveness Reflection Questions.

1. If there is any one thing to sum up our entire Christian faith, it is forgiveness. Christianity revolves around the hub of forgiveness. The foundation of our faith is forgiveness. The symbol of our faith is the cross upon which Christ died to grant us forgiveness. Our message is we can have our sins forgiven. Our call is to be forgiven and to forgive. Discuss what this means to you and your marriage?

2. Have you ever truly, without a doubt, received the forgiveness of God for your sin(s)? Share with your spouse when this was, or if you have not, ask Him to forgive you based on His life, death and resurrection for you.

3. If we are going to be like Jesus, we must forgive like Him. Not forgiving is a sin. How does this apply in your marriage?

4. Joe said, "Marriages do have major crises. However, in my experience it isn't a large problem which ends the relationship. It is how we respond to the large and small problems. We do not forgive each other." Do you agree or disagree? Why?

5. How would this principle improve your relationship: "The moment you are sinned against, hurt, wronged, or whatever phrase you use to describe it, in that moment, give forgiveness. Do not wait until they

know they sinned. Do not wait for them to confess or ask for forgiveness. Forgive them instantly the moment you realize they wronged you."

Sex Is A Big Deal

We turn the corner of this book and find ourselves at the corner of sex and awesome, or as I like to say, Awesome Sex.

If you are a man and reading this, I want to encourage you to stop and go read the first part of this book now. Great sex flows from a great relationship and it will not happen without one.

If you are a woman reading this, I have a word for you. Sex, for your husband, is far more important than you understand. Denise and I have been married since 1984. We have an incredible relationship, great sex, and open communication. We teach on this subject. We do counseling. We do sex counseling. In all of this, I still cannot fully describe to her how important sex is to a man. Actually, one thing more important than sex is this: my wife wanting to have and enjoying sex. To a man, the only thing we want more than great and frequent sex is for our wives to want great and frequent sex. My wife wanting me sexually does more for my perception of myself than just about anything else. She can be willing to have sex, and that is great. However, if she wants, not just willing, but wants it, that makes me feel important and greatly loved. Sex, when she initiates, is the best sex.

Sex is the major part of who we are, not just as individuals, but also as a culture. Think for a moment about the entire LBGTetc movement. We actually define our identity by who we want to have sex with! Heterosexual, homosexual, lesbian, bisexual, etc. Think about that. More than our socio-economic status, or even ethnicity; more and more we identify ourselves by the object of our sexual attraction. I do not tell you my socio-economic level or even my ethnicity. I define myself, my identity, by the object of my sexual attraction. People will define themselves by saying, "I have same sex attraction". Maybe I tell you I am a homosexual or lesbian. I give you a pronoun to let you know about my sexual identity. These are just ways of saying the gender of the person I desire sexually. Sex is such an important aspect that the object of my sexual attention is my very identity. I view myself and want others to view me based on the object of my sexual desires. This is huge. It really illustrates the power of sexuality.

Let's look for a few moments at sex. Just the act of sex and why I believe your sex life is both a sign of your real health and a product of a healthy relationship. It is a cause and effect. In my personal counseling ministry, so this is only my experience, but I have never had to provide marriage counsel to a couple with a great sex life. The flip side is true as well. Every couple I have ever counseled had a poor sex life. As I talk to these couples, I believe our sex lives both give us a thermometer to measure our relationships, and a thermostat to actually improve our relationships. Great sex flows from a great relationship and leads to a great relationship.

First, God designed us to be sexual creatures. Sex is the first command God gave to humanity after He created us. He made Adam and Eve and said:

'Be fruitful and multiply…" (Genesis 1:28)

This is a command to have sex. Think about it for a few moments. Really stop reading after this paragraph and digest the material. God created Adam. He created Eve and introduced her to Adam. Then, the first words God said to the first couple were an order to have a lot of sex. Sex is the only way to have children. You can not have a lot of children without a lot of sex. You cannot be fruitful and fill the earth without a lot of sex over a long period. God said, "Adam meet Eve. You two have a lot of sex."

Even as I type this, it seems strange. We are so conditioned to have a negative view of sexuality that the idea of God telling us to have a lot of sex seems weird. It isn't. God designed us with sex and sexuality, not just in mind, but in the forefront of our creation.

Not only is sex the first command given to humanity by God, sex is the first descriptive activity of humanity together. Before Eve, Adam named the animals. After God created Eve, He said for this reason they should cleave together and become one flesh. This is both emotional and physical. The one flesh relationship is never seen more than the act of sex.

"For this reason a man shall leave his father and his mother, and be joined to his wife; and they shall become one flesh. And the man and his wife were both naked, but they were not ashamed." (Genesis 2:24-25)

Once more, it is good to stop and consider the importance of these two things in order to understand the importance of sex and sexuality. God made a man and part of the creation is a penis. God gave Adam a penis and hormones designed to arouse. God created man with a sexual drive. The sexual drive placed into man is perhaps the strongest physical urge we possess. God created Adam with special nerves whose only function is pleasure and muscles whose only purpose is to produce an erection.

Then God created Eve. He created Eve with a vagina. He gave her hormones to produce arousal and cause the vagina to become moist and slick. He gave her specific pleasure centers and nerves as well. God designed Eve in such a way that if she were to take part in sex, it would bring her pleasure and orgasm.

God created orgasms. Consider that. God designed orgasms and put into the fabric of humanity. He made us so that there is only one way to have this specific explosion of pleasure. He wanted us to enjoy sex and made us with that in His mind. His purpose was for married couples to have orgasms together. It is not an accident. It is a design!

He then brought Eve to Adam and told them to have sex. Adam saw Eve and something happened. His penis became erect and hard. He felt a certain desire for the first time. He wanted to join her. Eve saw Adam and desired him. She felt warmth between her legs as he pulled him to her. They had sex.

If you received any form of discomfort reading the above few paragraphs, why? It was biologically written. It isn't any form of pornography. It is a simple description of how things occurred. God created humanity with the ability to derive pleasure from sex and then told them to have it. Adam met Eve and shortly thereafter they had sex. Do not overlook the truth that God created humanity with the ability and desire to enjoy sex. Sexuality is not part of the fall. It is part of the creation.

Sex is hard-wired by God into our biological design. Sex is the first command.

It is the first description of the first couple's life together. Human sexuality is important to God.

Another reason sex is so important is it is a holy act. Read that sentence again. Sex is a holy event. This is a surprise for many people. We have an almost dirty view of sex. In the best-case scenario, it is 'not bad'. Look at Hebrews 13.

"Marriage is to be held in honor among all, and the marriage bed is to be undefiled; for God will judge the sexually immoral and adulterers." (Hebrews 13:4)

There are two important words in this passage. The first is the phrase, "Marriage bed". This is the word we get coitus from. It is talking about sex. Married sex is the subject. This passage uses a word rarely used in the Bible. It is the word 'undefiled'. It is used to describe the holy nature of Jesus Christ Himself. God uses the same word to describe marriage sex. Sex outside of marriage is sinful. Sex inside of a marriage is an act of holiness so pure God uses the same word to describe Himself.

Holy means far more than not doing something bad. We redefined it to mean that in evangelical Christianity. We think holy is 'not being bad'. You can 'not be bad' without being good. They are not opposites. In the Scriptures, holiness means to be set apart for God to use you in the accomplishment of His will. God uses holy people to accomplish holy goals. If I am holy, then I line my life up with the purposes and plan of God and I am submissive to Him working in and through me. This applies to married sex. It is holy. I am the holy instrument of God uniquely created by Him to provide intense and holy pleasure to my wife. When I have sex with her, I am being used by God. It is holy. I challenge the reader to meditate on this passage and interpretation for a bit. When I have sex with my wife, I am being used by God to provide holy pleasure to her. When my wife has sex with me, she is serving God as well. Sex is holy. We honor God as we have sex with our spouses. The act of sex within a marriage is a holy activity bringing honor to the Father. The marriage bed (the act of sex) is set apart for God to use. It is holy.

Satan caused us to think the exact opposite. We view sex in a marriage as, at best, not a sinful thing. We think of sex in a marriage as acceptable. God permits it. He allows us to have sex, so we won't sin. This gives us a negative view of sexuality. God designed sex and marriage to bring Him glory as He uses us to give holy pleasure to one of His children. Married sex is not merely an acceptable act God allows us to do. It is holy and good act He commands us to perform.

The truth that sex within marriage is holy and sex outside of marriage is sinful reveals another important truth of human sexuality. Notice this passage speaks of two types of sexual encounters. The first is within a marriage. The other is outside of the marriage. God places morality upon them. The one inside the marriage is holy and brings Him honor. Sex outside of marriage is sinful and will be judged. This truth comes in direct conflict with culture. Sex is a moral act. It is more than biological. It is moral. Sex itself possesses morality. Therefore, the modern sexual revolution glorifying sexuality without parameters is wrong.

Most people will admit there is some degree of sexual morality. Hollywood, with the low standard it maintains, is adamantly against the 'casting couch' or folks in power leveraging sexual favors for their benefit. Everyone views sex without consent as wrong. Sex with children is wrong. People place morality upon sexuality. The problem is their moral standard is subjective and open. They do not have a moral standard to determine the morality of it. The knowledge ingrained in us, leading us to place some moral parameters on sexuality, reveal to us sex is a moral (or immoral) act. We all agree it should somehow be regulated in some way. We all agree some sex is in and of itself wrong. The very fact we know it has limits indicates some standard outside of ourselves. Our Creator gave that standard to us. God teaches us sex is not just biological, but moral. He also gives us the standard. It is simple.

"Marriage is to be held in honor among all, and the marriage bed is to be undefiled; for God will judge the sexually immoral and adulterers." (Hebrews 13:4)

Sex within a marriage is holy and good. Sex outside of marriage is sin. Period. We don't need to define the age of consent, or when a person can or cannot, or with whom a person can have sex. God answers all those questions. Sex in a marriage is pure and holy. Anything else is not.

So far we have seen:

Sex is so important it was part of the first conversation and command between God and humanity.

We see lovemaking as one of the first activities of humanity.

God biologically designed sex and sexuality into our humanity for procreation and recreation.

Sex is holy. Sexual intimacy in marriage is more than permitted by God. It is a holy act.

Sex is moral. There is a moral standard behind and within it.

Another thing to consider as we dive into human sexuality is the truth that sex is mystical. Somehow, sex is not just a physical activity. It is spiritual in nature.

Before explaining this, first we need to realize it is impossible to take part in any spiritual activity without your physical input. You cannot pray, fast, meditate, give, sacrifice, or study Scripture without using your physical body and aspects of your physical nature. Whether it is merely our minds, physical brains, giving focused attention, or our hands handing water to the thirsty, physical and spiritual flow together. God intertwined our spiritual and physical lives in an inseparable connection. Sin, a spiritual offense, happens in and with the body. Any action of holiness or good occurs in the body. This applies to sex as well. Our sexual behavior is a physical and a spiritual event. I do not understand it. I simply see it in Scripture.

Various times in the Old Testament, God referred to the sin of Israel as committing adultery. 1 Corinthians 6:15-20 speaks of sexual sin.

"Do you not know that your bodies are parts of Christ? Shall I then take away the parts of Christ and make them parts of a prostitute? Far from it! Or do you not know that the one who joins himself to a prostitute is one body with her? For He says, "The two shall become one flesh." But the one who joins himself to the Lord is one spirit with Him. Flee sexual immorality. Every other sin that a person commits is outside the body, but the sexually immoral person sins against his own body. Or do you not know that your body is a temple of the Holy Spirit within you, whom you have from God, and that you are not your own? For you have been bought for a price: therefore glorify God in your body."

We should not sin sexually because the Holy Spirit is inside of us and we are one with Him. We should not be one with a prostitute and the Lord. We must glorify God in our body because the Holy Spirit is inside of us. All of this is tied to the mystical nature of sex. Sexual integrity is specifically connected to our spiritual nature and connection with God.

In Ephesians 5, where God is speaking of Christ, He quotes the Scripture about man and woman in Genesis.

"So husbands also ought to love their own wives as their own bodies. He who loves his own wife loves himself; for no one ever hated his own flesh, but nourishes and cherishes it, just as Christ also does the church, because we are parts of His body. For this reason a man shall leave his father and his mother and be joined to his wife, and the two shall become one flesh. This mystery is great; but I am speaking with reference to Christ and the church."

Notice the mystery of Christ and the church is referred to in the one-flesh sex statement. We, the church, are part of His body. In order to show how important it is for a man to love His wife, God refers to the mystical nature of Christ and the church and then ties it to sexuality. The act of sex in a marriage is actually an illustration of the love Christ has for the church.

Is it any wonder the enemy of our souls wants to confuse us, attack us, or distort our understanding of human sexuality? It is hard-wired into our being so much that confusion on sexuality leads to confusion of life. Today, in my opinion, the single greatest challenge of the evangelical church in America is culture's competing view of human sexuality. Anyone born after 1990 struggles with the Biblical teaching sex is limited to one man and one woman in a marriage. Virtually no one under 40 believes this truth. Sexuality is fluid in their opinions and beliefs. I believe this is a success story of Satan, and the only way to combat it is through truth and love.

In virtually every single counseling session I have had, people struggled with this understanding of human sexuality. Satan distorted and perverted it to such a degree we have trouble envisioning the original.

God created sex.

God created orgasms.

God wants us to give great sex to each other.

Sex is wonderful and honors Him.

It is mystical and moral, beautiful and mysterious.

It is interwoven into our being.

We long to give and receive great sex.

In your marriage, having wonderful sex honors
God.

It stands to reason if God created us to have sex, then having sex is a good thing. It is a proven good. We benefit from having sex in every area of our lives. If you have frequent sex, you are likely to have benefits from lower blood pressure to a lower divorce rate. Sexual frequency and intimacy are life transforming. Studies show sex in a one man/one woman relationship increases your emotional connection with each other. The hormones released in sex are specifically designed to enhance your sense of bonding and belonging. A healthy sex life spills over to other areas and increases a commitment to improving the relationships. Here are a few reasons to step up your sex game in your marriage. A great resource for sexual information is www.verywellmind.com. I got some of this information from there.

Frequent sex has psychological benefits. I mentioned

earlier, after all these years, Denise still doesn't understand how much I want her to want sex. Part of that is rooted in self image. A great sex life will boost your own self-perceptions and give you a good self-esteem. It leads to a positive self image. Studies show people who have frequent sex are happier. When you make love, your brain releases endorphins which increase your feelings of happiness, calmness and contentment. It also releases and decreases feelings of stress in your life. Turn this upside down and re-read it, replacing your spouse as the recipient of these things. If I have a lot of sex with Denise, I can help her self image and give her a better and more positive attitude. I can help her be happier and decrease stress in her life. Good sex, and frequent sex, will give her feelings of happiness, calmness, and contentment. Remember, love is not selfish. I should seek these things for her and the way I can give them to here is through frequent sex.

We live in a culture of people obsessed with physical fitness, weight loss and health. Even the vast majority of people who are not in good shape know they should be and plan on 'one day' getting healthy. A great place to start is to have a lot of sex. According to the American Heart Association, sexual activity is equal to climbing two flights of stairs. Repetitive sex can tone abdominal muscles and even improve bladder control. My wife says she wishes her fitbit had a sexometer like the pedometer so she could get credit for the exercise. A thirty minute sexual encounter burns 200 calories and releases hormones which help in weight loss. The cardio involved decreases blood pressure and increases oxygen delivery throughout the body. Sex is physically good for you.

More frequent intercourse leads to improved memory performance and improves one's immune system. People who have a lot of sex are less likely to become ill. The same endorphins are also linked to a reduction in back pain and decreases your chance of migraine headaches. For a woman, frequent intercourse is associated with less painful menstrual periods.

Sex is a Big Deal Reflection Questions

1. The emphasis of the book is our love relationship and our sex relationship are interdependent. A great love relationship produces a great sex life and a great sex life leads to a great relationship. Joe said he has never had to give prolonged marriage counsel to a couple who had a great sex life. He also said he has never known a couple with a great relationship who did not have wonderful sex. Talk about this. If your daily relationship is interdependent upon your sexual intimacy, and vice/versa...does this shed light on anything in your marriage?

2. Men talk about this quote with your wife. "To a man, the only thing we want more than great and frequent sex is for our wives to want great and frequent sex. My wife wanting me sexually does more for my perception of myself than just about anything else."

3. Talk about each main point in this initial chapter. Discuss it, agree/disagree, thoughts, ideas or applications.

a. Sex is so important it was part of the first conversation and command between God and humanity.

b. We see lovemaking was one of the first activities of the human race.

c. Sex and sexuality are biologically designed into our

humanity and not only allow procreation but recreation as well.

d. Sex is holy. Sexual intimacy in marriage is more than permitted by God. It is a holy act.

e. Sex is moral. It is not merely some biological drive. There is a moral standard behind and within it.

f. Sex is mystical. Somehow, in some way, sex is not just a physical activity. It is spiritual in nature.

Roadblocks To Great Sex

I want to reiterate how important sex within a marriage is to our relationship. I said earlier, after almost forty years of completely open communication, Denise still does not fully understand how much sex means to men. A wife initiating sex is one of the greatest joys for a husband. A wife declining sex is one of the greatest hurts. Turning sex down can be more demoralizing and discouraging than many wives realize. Because of this, we need to spend time on why so many couples have issues with sexuality and sex in marriages.

I believe one of the reasons is we have a poor worldview of sex. We do not understand the Biblical teaching of sex. I addressed this in the previous chapter. In place of having a Biblical worldview of sex, we put other misunderstandings that guide our perceptions. The first one is that sex is bad or neutral. This is a big one to overcome especially in Christian circles. Culture's focus on sexual freedom has caused the church to overreact in its presentation of purity. Sexual purity is emphasized in the church. We constantly teach "NO" when it comes to sex. We don't always balance that with how good sex inside of a marriage is. More often than not churches, by accident or on purpose, portray sex as a bad thing to be avoided more than a good thing to be embraced. Sex can be a hard subject to discuss, so in our churches and in our families, often it seems easier if we just don't talk about it or we talk the prohibitions of it. We find it easier to discuss how sex is wrong outside of a marriage of a husband and a wife, than it is to discuss the benefits of a good sex life. We have fallen into the trap of only talking about the negative side of sex. We discuss putting up barriers and protections.

My wife and I have homeschooled for over thirty years. Part of the homeschooling subculture has been the courtship movement and purity rings. It is all about how wicked and bad sex is. This is true for sex outside of marriage. We have neglected the rest of the teaching on how great sex is inside of marriage. So, here is what happens. We indoctrinate our children on the evil of sex. Sexual sin is one of the 'ultimate' sins we seek to prevent. A much greater emphasis is placed on sexual sin as opposed to the sins of greed, the desire to be rich, a gluttonous desire for food, speaking evil of others, or judging others. We might ignore the great commission and the great commandment, however, we must fight sexual sin. We portray sex and sexual desire as evil. Young girls cannot even dress in certain manners because it will tempt those poor boys to lust. BTW, I hate the way we blame girls for boy's sin.

We as Christian parents and churches teach that sex is bad, sexual desire is bad, sexual attention is bad, dressing sexually is bad. Then after a twenty-minute service and an exchange of rings and vows, we expect our young married couples to have a healthy view of sex and have sex frequently. After a lifetime of sex being addressed with negative connotations and consequences, how can my worldview and thought process go from evil to good because we ate a piece of cake in front of a bunch of people and are now married? Denise and I, just this week while driving, listened to a series on sexuality for churches and parents to teach to their children. The presenter used the word "Sexual Integrity" instead of sexual purity. I like that.

The idea is to have a solid worldview of sex, which integrates seamlessly into our lives as followers of Jesus. Sex is not bad. It is bad if not done Biblically. Sex is good. We started this study on sexuality with our two children who still live at home. Sex is not evil. Sexual desire is not evil. Sexual desire and sex are a wonderful part of who God created us to be. We simply need to maintain integrity and have sex the way our loving Creator designed for it to be.

Another erroneous idea is that sex is for men. Culture presents men in as sexual predators and insatiable monsters. All men want to do is have sex. Women can have sex, but men must have it. This makes the control of sex by the woman a means of controlling and dominating a man. It makes men into beggars who only want some crumbs. In this view, sex becomes a tool by either the man or the woman to manipulate the relationship. Men are seen as too aggressive and women are seen as too passive. Sex itself is a means of manipulation.

The idea that sex is about me also permeates and destroys our sexuality and the enjoyment of sex in our marriage. I will speak to this more in the next chapter, but for now, let me say this. As God's holy instrument in the act of sex, you are to seek the pleasure of your spouse. It is not a selfish act of gratification. It is a giving act of pleasure and love which virtually always results in your own pleasure as well. The point is, the focus is not selfish. It is giving.

Our sexual past can also hurt our sex lives. This is especially true for victims of sexual abuse. The weaponizing of sex, the pain, and the consequences it causes those who have been wrongfully used for sexual pleasure is extremely difficult to overcome. Denise speaks to this occasionally. She was the victim of sexual assault and trauma as a child. Shortly after we were married, we went to seek counseling. The reason was straightforward. Denise struggled with flashbacks, emotional pain, and memories of horrible abuse that flooded back into her mind every time we had sex. The fact she was now married to me and I was not the one who hurt her did not change her emotions. She still associated sex with feelings of pain, 'dirtiness', guilt, fear, and shame. It is extremely difficult to go from such a dark pit of ugliness to a feeling of purity in sex. She loved me and even had a sexual desire for me, but the past agony associated with sex affected our current relationship. For victims of sexual assault the challenges can be ongoing even if it was in the distant past. Understandably, many victims fall on a spectrum of using sex as form of control so as to never be hurt by it again to a complete aversion to it. Most victims are somewhere in between. If you or your spouse have been the victim of a sexual assault, and it is affecting your current sex life, I encourage you to seek good counsel. There is help available. Maybe it won't be the first answer you get or the first person you speak to (it wasn't for us), but help is available. Overcoming Denise's past hurts took time and discipline on her part as she retrained her thinking, as well as compassion, sensitivity, and tenderness on my part. It also took hours of open and honest communication. Sexual assault is an ugly crime and it has ugly consequences, but Jesus is all powerful and all healing and can heal the deepest of wounds. God wants to redeem the past that satan meant for evil and to transform it into something for your good and for your benefit.

Sexual shame also causes roadblocks to great sex. The accuser of the brethren will tempt us with sexual sin. If in your past you succumbed to the temptation and had sexual encounters before or outside of marriage, satan will use the sin of your past to attempt to hurt you in the present. He uses shame, guilt and remorse to cast a shadow on what is now holy sex. It is also a way he uses to cast doubt on our spouses. In my pre-marriage counseling, I tell couples this.

"If you will violate God's standard before you are married, why won't you break it after? The standard is the same. It is sex inside of marriage that is holy before God. You broke it then. Why would you not break it now? If you will have sex with each other outside of marriage, then why would they not have sex with another outside of marriage? If physical and emotional attraction were all it took for you to break God's standard, then what will keep you from breaking it again if you are physically or emotionally attracted to someone?"

These are the thoughts satan will put into your mind, or your spouse's mind. The enemy of our soul will use the shame of your past to cloud your present and overshadow your joy. You can overcome the shame and guilt through repentance and Calvary. You do not overcome sexual shame or sin by marriage. I tell couples during premarital counseling, "Getting married will not forgive your past sexual sin. It makes all sex afterwards good and holy, but your sin still stains the relationship. Only Jesus can forgive sexual sin. The blood of Christ applied to our confessing and repenting of sin defeats it."

It is not just our worldview which causes roadblocks to

great sex. It is simply life. One huge problem is exhaustion. I know the act of sex is not really a big physical event. The average time sex takes for a married couple is not long from first kiss to cleanup. Long periods of lovemaking are the exception and not the rule. Yet, we are too tired because of the pace of our lives. We live with little or no margin and rarely relax. We go to bed stressed out by our day and experiencing pre-game stress for tomorrow. Our list of activities and tasks done and to do are overwhelming. I am not necessarily physically exhausted, I am mentally and emotionally done. I am the stereotypical horny husband and many nights I have gone to bed hoping my wife would not initiate sex. I just did not want to do it. I was too tired. I have an office job. I do not physically exert myself, ever. Life itself, with no margin and no stopping point, wears us out. It is not the actual physical activity of sex. It is the emotional focus good sex requires. I do not want to do that. I want to sleep.

This goes along with exhaustion. We have too much stress in our lives. We push ourselves to the limits in our careers, parenting, activities, church volunteering, enjoyment, etc. We are always doing something with something else waiting to be done. We have a queue of important activities waiting to be done. We have relational stress, financial stress, family stress, health stress, and time stress. We are all stressed up with nowhere to go. This constant stress makes it difficult to clear our minds and focus on the sexual pleasure of our spouse. Even sex becomes another stress. I should have it but don't want to. That stresses me out. Denise once told me she had to overcome parenting stress in order to be a sexual wife.

She said, "All day long people touch me. It is non-stop. The kids are around me, holding me, putting hands on me, talking to me, needing me, and did I say, touching me? I just want to go to bed and not have anyone need or touch me for a short time. I just don't want to be touched physically or mentally. Then, you obviously want to do both and it is a struggle for me. Parenting hurts my sex life."

We find another significant roadblock in how men and women are wired differently. I call it instant sex. Good sex generally needs to have a buildup to it. This includes, but isn't limited to, foreplay. My wife says women need a moment to at least wake up. A man can walk into the room and see his wife lying in the bed and be instantly aroused and want sex. He wakes up in the morning with a typical morning erection and decides to use it. He walks into the room as his wife is changing into her pajamas and gets immediately aroused. Women need, in Denise's words, "Time to reorient and stop our mental task list. Women need a moment to disengage from the mental activity of life." She also says that many times instant sex feels selfish. The man sees his wife, becomes aroused, and wants gratification. There is no intimacy. There are a lot of instant sex moments in marriage. However, if this is the total of your sex life, it creates a roadblock because of the lack of intimate time.

Another roadblock to great sex is magnified when children enter the family. Privacy is paramount. Couples are worried their children will see or hear them. This doesn't change. I am nearly sixty years old. Recently my adult children spent the night with us. They were in the living room playing a video game. Our bedroom shares a wall with the living room. I initiated sex. Denise said, "Not now. They might hear us." Now, we did their premarital counseling. We talked a lot about sex in it. They know we have a healthy sex life. We have shown physical affection in front of them their entire lives. We are open about holy sex. We have eleven children. Our family has a shared chat group called "Married Holmans" and in it we often post funny sexual jokes, memes, and things from the web. Nothing pornographic or vulgar, just sex related humor. My 33-year-old son knows his parents do it. They also had the volume turned up so loud we could hear the game and their laughter. Add to that fact, our sex rarely involves loud noises. None of this mattered. Denise could not feel aroused knowing there was the smallest chance our kids might know we were doing it. My point is simple. Married sex should be a private event. If privacy isn't assured, then we divert part of our attention to security guard detail. The best sex is often when we feel the most comfortable and secure.

One other quick note on this subject of privacy. Please keep your sexual encounters between yourself and your spouse. Many a husband or a wife feels violated when they hear their spouse speak publicly about their sex life. I am not talking about mutually agreed upon discussion in order to help others in their marriage and in their sex lives as we are trying to do in this book. I am talking about just casually injecting into conversation something that should be kept between you and your spouse. I admonish you to keep your love life private. It is some unique and exclusive between the two of you.

The final roadblock I want to mention is the greatest one in my opinion. I have mentioned it before and will mention it again. You will never have better sex than your non-sexual relationship. If your relationship is full of criticism, correction, complaining, anger, unforgiveness, bitterness, hurt, lack of communication, etc., then your sexual life will reflect it. In counseling, I often use a simple diagram of a ratio. It is a direct proportion. The deeper your relationship, the better your sex. The inverse is true as well. A mediocre to poor relationship causes a poor to bad sex life. Sex is an expression and buildup of all day, week, month long love.

Removing the roadblocks.
I don't want to just end this chapter with a list of roadblocks. Let's take a minute and knock them down.

Roadblock: Erroneous worldview about human sexuality and sex.
Solution: Read the book again, slowly. :)

Roadblock: Bad relationship.
Solution: The first half of this book. Make your relationship with your spouse the single most important thing in your life.

Roadblock: Worry about privacy.
Solution: Put a lock on your door. Play soft music all the time so kids always hear it and not just 'sometimes'. Take practical steps to ensure it is just the two of you and will be just the two of you. We not only lock the door, I put something in front of it so it cannot be opened without force.

Roadblock: Only instant sex.

Solution: Plan for romantic dates culminating in sex. Go to hotels, give massages, give yourself foreplay time restrictions. If you are suddenly aroused, start slowly leading up to it. Do not have morning sex unless you have time for morning after sex relaxing.

Roadblock: Sexual selfishness.

Solution: Seek the fulfillment of your spouse in all things. Put their needs and desires above your own. It is more important for my spouse to feel fulfilled than it is for me to feel fulfilled.

Roadblock: Sexual assault or abuse in your past

Solution: Seek counseling to learn how to heal from your past sexual abuse. Forgive the one(s) who hurt you. Learn how to communicate and express how your sexual trauma has impacted you in the present. Move forward toward a positive view of sex and a healthy sex life with your spouse. Spouses of one who was abused, love them the way you would want to be loved. Take it slow. Show compassion and empathy.

Roadblock: Sexual guilt and shame from your own sexual activity in the past.

Solution: Seek forgiveness for your sin and trust God granted it.

Roadblock: Stress and exhaustion.

Solution: Learn to put plenty of margin in your life. Do not live from one thing to another. Schedule and maintain down time, sabbaths, sabbaticals, days off, time to chill, etc. Life is not about doing more all the time.

Roadblocks To Great Sex Reflection Questions

1. Go over each of the roadblocks below and discuss them. Is this something you need to work on in your relationship? Go over each solution to the roadblocks and work out a plan to implement them in your sex life.

a) Non-Biblical worldview which leads to a 'necessary evil' conclusion about sex.

b) Sex is for men not women. Men must have it, women can if they choose.

c) Sex is to gratify my desires.

d) Sexual hurt such as abuse or misuse in your past.

e) Sexual shame from past sin.

f) Living on the edge of exhaustion due to no margin.

g) Stressed out life.

h) The different 'wiring' of men and women in the sexual area.

i) Children

j) Privacy concerns

k) Poor non-sexual relationship.

How To Have Great Sex

We often refer to sex as making love. I love this terminology. I also like love making. I think both are true. Love makes sex great. Love making. Great sex improves our relationship, or making love. Love makes sex and sex makes love. This is why it is impossible to stress the first half of this book too much. You want to have sex with your best friend! Make him/her your best friend in every sense of the word.

In total honesty, I truly believe the reason we have such a wonderful sexual relationship is because our friendship and love outside of sexuality is so incredible. What happens in the bedroom is simply an expression of life outside of it.

So, let's assume from this point on, you and your husband/wife are in a wonderful place in your marriage relationship. You are, as my dad used to say, firing on all cylinders. The truth is, good lovemaking is an outflow of a relationship and it is a learned skill. What does it take to have wonderful sex?

The first step is to look at the roadblocks, the obstacles to sex, and remove or overcome them. We have touched on a few in the previous chapter, but you might even have other roadblocks that we didn't mention. Seek to remove any roadblocks to great sex with your best friend.

The next way to have awesome sex is simple. Is is like the old saying says, "Practice makes perfect." When we were learning Spanish as missionaries in Bolivia, our language teacher said, "The only way to learn another language is to make a million mistakes." She emphasized practice. We learn to play a musical instrument through small steps and hours of practice. Every learned skill you possess, from learning to walk as a child to the most advanced thing you can achieve, was learned little by little, step by step. This same thing is true for sex. The worst sex of our lives was our honeymoon. It was great at the time, but it was insecure and without knowledge. We had no practice nor time to improve our skill.

The way to have great sex is to learn it by having a lot of not great sex. Practice makes perfect. It is also God's plan for you. I do not mean the 'not great' part of that sentence. The 'having a lot' part. Look at 1 Corinthians 7.

Now concerning the things about which you wrote, it is good for a man not to touch a woman. But because of sexual immoralities, each man is to have his own wife, and each woman is to have her own husband. The husband must fulfill his duty to his wife, and likewise the wife also to her husband. The wife does not have authority over her own body, but the husband does; and likewise the husband also does not have authority over his own body, but the wife does. Stop depriving one another, except by agreement for a time so that you may devote yourselves to prayer, and come together again so that Satan will not tempt you because of your lack of self-control. (1 Corinthians 7:1-5)

The first phrase where is states 'not to touch a woman' is a Greek phrase speaking to arousal. God, in line with the teaching of lust equals adultery, says we should not sexually arouse another person. However, He created us to arouse and be aroused, therefore we should get married in order to meet each other's needs. He then goes on and says each member of the marriage is in control of the sexual frequency in the marriage. I teach this in pre-marriage counseling. In a nutshell, God is telling the wife to have sex with her husband whenever he wants to have it. The same thing is true for the husband. He is to make love to his wife on demand. This sounds politically incorrect at first. However, when you factor in the Bible as a whole, and our entire love relationship, then I will not insist my spouse have sex if she really doesn't want to. The same goes for her. She has the right for me to have sex with her even if I don't feel in the mood. We are not speaking to our entitlement to use the Bible to make each of us 'submit' to the other. We are saying that each of you should joyfully choose to serve the other and meet their needs as a holy act. If she doesn't have a legitimate reason to not give her love to me sexually, then she should make love. The same is true for me. The truth is, choosing to joyfully make love when you do not feel like it is actually a deeper expression of love than having sex when you want to do it. Again, this is true for both the husband and the wife. You are both to joyfully serve the other sexually anytime you spouse desires, unless you can say before God there is a reason not to do it.

Denise and I tell couples, "In a marriage, there are no 'No's'. However, there are no selfish demands, either." Please understand this. We are saying that 'yes' should be your default setting and mentality when you know your spouse desires to make love to you. However, do not misunderstand what we are saying. Demanding my way is the least effective and least relationship building way to get my way in the bedroom and in life. In parenting, we tell parents that perhaps there might be a very few times in your entire parenting career you will say, "Because I am your parent and I said so". However, appealing to this 'because I say so' method, is the not the way you want your children to comply to you and do what you ask. You want them to love you and to desire to please you out of your RELATIONSHIP with them, not because of your authority over them. They trust, love and respect you and those cause them to want to comply with your requests because they know that you want the absolute best for them. The same is true in the husband/wife relationship. Yes, we each have God given authority over the other one's body as seen in the verses above. But as loving spouses we want to rarely, if ever, appeal to that authority. In a healthy, loving relationship there is not a need to demand anything, because there is mutual love and respect and a desire to serve the other one. This is why we began with the relationship focus in entire first half of the book.

Now back to practice makes perfect. Have a lot of sex. Some think this is a great idea and others, because of an erroneous worldview, think it is a bad one. I believe in our society women are programmed to think men all men want is sex and they want it selfishly and constantly. As I type this, two of my grandchildren are watching one of the Ice Age cartoons. The wooly mammoths just had a conversation in which the female told the male she would never mate with him. Of course, it goes over the heads of little children, but the portrayal of demand and denial, control and manipulation, male desire and female rejection is such a part of culture it is in a kid's cartoon. We buy into it. The wife thinks if she always agrees to sex, then they will have sex every day and maybe even more than once a day.

So, where is the bad in that? Why would making love every day be a bad thing if the two of you become so good at it that it provides you with one of the greatest pleasures in life? However, that is not what will happen. Men and women both have limits. Here is an example. On three occasions my wife and I have taken the one month challenge. The goal is to have sex at least once a day for an entire month. Yep, thirty times in one month. What happens is by day ten, I am struggling. My little biological factory cannot keep up with demand. The testosterone plant is working overtime and output is exceeding capability. And honestly I just get tired of having sex every day. Some nights I just want to go to sleep. We are sex counselors. We believe in human sexuality and the inherent goodness of it. We. Love. Sex. Yet, we have never made it past 18 days. In every case, I was the one who tapped out. I just did not want to. Men are not insatiable. The stereotype is not accurate.

Your sex drive also decreases as you go through hormonal changes in life and as you age. I am approaching 60. Denise and I went on a cruise together for my 59th birthday and I told her I wanted, a phrase we coined a while back, a sexcation and not a vacation. We have done these in the past. We plan on making love every day and often more than once a day. I could not do it. After the third day and fourth time, I had to wait for two days. The spirit was willing, but the flesh was weak. So, let me give advice to younger couples. Go for it. Have a lot of sex. It helps to build your relationship and one day you will not have the same stamina…although it honestly gets better with age. I told Denise, "I know I am slowly losing the physical ability to make love. So, I want to have as much as I can while I can."

This same passage, 1 Corinthians 7, adds another thing. God tells us we cannot deprive each other. This is strong language. God, our Creator and Redeemer, our Lord and King, tells us to meet the sexual needs of our spouse and to not do so is harmful. The only acceptable time to not have routine and regular sex is when you both agree to a timeframe in order to devote yourselves to prayer and fasting. God says having regular and consistent sex that not having it opens a path for Satan to tempt us. He also says only deep prayer and fasting are the only legitimate reasons to interrupt regular lovemaking.

This is in such contrast to the erroneous stereotype, or the better word for it is lie, about God and sex. Satan convinced us that God is against sex. We look at sex as a guilty pleasure used by Satan. I had a person tell me one time her pastor taught the 'fruit' in the garden was sex. He taught his church sex was the original sin. The Catholic Church, among others, elevates chastity and virginity to a super spiritual level and demand leadership possess both. The truth is God created sex and commands us to have a lot of it. Jesus said not many people have been given the gift of chastity, therefore the vast majority of us should get married. We are wired to be sexual beings. So, the first way to become awesome in your lovemaking together is to make love. Again and again and again.

Whenever we counsel people, there is one Biblical principle we stress in relationships and our sexual lives.

"(Love) does not seek its own benefit... (1 Corinthians 13:5)

"Do nothing from selfishness or empty conceit, but with humility consider one another as more important than yourselves; do not merely look out for your own personal interests, but also for the interests of others.." (Philippians 2:3-4)

"Give preference to one another in honor." (Romans 12:10)

Go back to our definition of holiness as applied to sex within our marriage. I am to be set apart in order for God to use me to provide intimate pleasure to my spouse. Sexual holiness means I want God to use me for fulfilling my husband/wife. One of the biggest problems people face in a marriage is selfishness. If we are selfish in our marriage, then our focus is on what I receive from this relationship and not what I can give to it. I keep a mental input/output record in my mind and demand the ratio of what I receive is equal to or greater than the input I give. This is the opposite of Biblical Christianity and destroys relationships. It also radically harms our sexual lives. Many times, lovemaking is little more than legalized prostitution. Sex is leveraged to manipulate our spouses and/or we, especially women, feel used instead of loved. Twice women told us in counseling that they could easily be replaced with an inflatable sex doll. The saying, "Wam, Bam, thank you Ma'am" is a horrible description of a sex life.

If you want to excel in making love, then seek to do

everything you can to please your partner. Learn what he/she likes and do it. Make their pleasure the goal and your pleasure a great by-product of it. Imagine this in action. Both the husband and the wife are doing their absolute best to maximize the experience and pleasure of their partner. I am not trying to have an orgasm. I am seeking to give my wife an incredible experience and an out-worldly orgasm. My goal is for this climax to be the best so far in her life. I promise you, along the road to this my needs will be fully met. Then, if she is doing the same thing, wow! Putting this one principle in place in your relationship and lovemaking will transform your sex life and your relationship outside of the bedroom too. Put the needs of the other person first. (Making) Love is not selfish, it does not seek its own.

In the first part of this book, I taught about communication. I said the number one skill we should develop in our relationship is to learn how to truly and deeply communicate. We seek to understand and empathize with each other. This skill is greatly advantageous in making love. When you understand the Biblical teaching of sex being good, and how the first couple were naked and unashamed, you can apply this to your married and sex lives. Talk to each other during sex. Speak words of love and appreciation. Say intimate things. Also, share with each other what you like, where, how and even why. Show each other what brings the greatest pleasure. Practice moves with a verbal input of encouragement and modification in order to make your activity more pleasurable. Replace assumptions with knowledge. I might think my wife enjoys it when I do a particular action. If I ask her, I can know for certain. We have done this through the years and many times, our assumptions were not completely accurate. Also, sometimes things we loved in the past do not bring us as much pleasure in the present. Our bodies and hormones change. Share this with your husband/wife. Ask them what you can do next for them. Ask which move feels better and what you can do to improve. Give multiple choice options. Do you like this? Or this? Or this? Which one is best?

Here is a great example. I stink. That is a fact. My physical makeup is such that my body produces more and worse odor than a normal person. Even as a teenager, my brothers called me "Stinkbutt" due to body odor. One time I could tell Denise was not enjoying herself as much and asked what was going on. She hesitantly confessed to me that my body odor was difficult to overcome. It is a fact.

So, here is what I do now. I take a shower every night before going to bed. I shave, use body wash and then one of her favorite colognes. I wash until I am squeaky clean. I go to bed, every single night, smelling good. If we are on vacation and I sense we are going to make love in the middle of the afternoon, I jump in the shower and do a quick stink-off of my body. I make it a point to be clean shaven and good smelling before any opportunity to make love. I could be offended, but why? She spoke honestly to me and I know it is true.

Guess what happened? On hundreds of occasions, I mean that, hundreds of times, I have gone to bed and my good smell turned her on. She was not planning on making love until I climbed in beside her, smelling clean and nice. The same sense, smell, which turned her off can turn her on.

This is just one little way we can improve our lovemaking by communication. After almost forty years of marriage, just today, Denise asked me to do something different than I typically do. My goal is her pleasure, so I did it. Talk, listen, share, and learn from each other. Be naked and not ashamed. Teach each other how to give pleasure. Stop assuming and start learning!

One final reflection, in your communication to one another about your sex life, be sensitive. You are talking about an extremely vulnerable part of your lives. It is deeply personal and as such we can easily hurt our life partner by conveying our thoughts in an unkind way. Remember all of the one-another of Scripture still apply and even more so here during these delicate conversations. Communicate your desires and your displeasures with kindness, gentleness, compassion, encouragement, and love. Speaking to your best friend as you wish to be spoken to.

This is connected to communication, but it is targeted to another Person. Pray. God is interested in your sex lives. He created them. He designed them. He wants to use you in the life of your spouse. So, pray. Ask Him to help you improve. In the early part of our marriage, I had premature ejaculation issues. I climaxed quickly and first. Denise and I talked about it and looked up ways to help me learn to control my orgasms. I also prayed. I asked God before and during lovemaking to help me. I asked for wisdom and self-control. I would pray for longevity and the Holy Spirit would advise me to slow down and or stop for a while to focus on Denise. I know this sounds strange, but that is because we do not have a Biblical worldview of sexuality. The truth that God designed and is interested in our sexual lives allows us to bring them before Him. Prayer is not some spiritual discipline limited to a quiet time. We are to pray without ceasing. To this day, I still pray often during sex. I pray for Denise to love it. I pray for, still, longevity. I pray for her to know I love her. Communicate with each other and with God.

The last thing for this chapter on improving your sex life is this. Relax and enjoy the journey. Sex is a journey. Enjoy the trip. Do not be uptight or worried. You are on the road together. Take your time. Enjoy it. Denise and I have been making love since 1984. Last night we talked about it. After over 38 years of lovemaking, we still put it number one on our list of fun things we do together and are still learning and seeking to improve. Your sexual life is not this one session of intercourse. This time of intimacy is just a small part of a lifetime of mutual pleasure. Enjoy each step.

How To Have Great Sex Reflection Questions

1. Joe said, "The way to have great sex is to learn it by having a lot of not great sex. Practice makes perfect. It is also God's plan for you. I do not mean the 'not great' part of that sentence. The 'having a lot' part." Read the first five verses of 1 Corinthians 7. Does it surprise you that God's will is for you to have a lot of sex?

2. In 1 Corinthians 7 we learn it is the will of God for the wife to meet the sexual needs of her husband and for him to meet hers. In other words, if we deprive each other sexually, we are in sin. It also plainly states withholding sex is only allowed for spiritual purposes, with a definite starting and ending point, and we must be careful or it opens the door for satan to tempt us. How does this fit into: (a)your current sex life; and (b) your historical understanding of sex in a marriage?

3. If the idea of making love often, several times a week, does not excite you, why? What is it about having sex that does not make it one of the greatest moments of your life? Be honest with each other (with kindness). The goal is to improve. If making love is one of your most incredible and satisfying experiences you will want to do it often. So, how can you improve?

4. Take the 30 day challenge. Try to have intercourse at least once a day for a month. Discuss your feelings

after each week. How is it going?

5. Applying the biblical definition of holiness, to be set apart for God to use you, to marriage means this: I am to be set apart in order for God to use me to provide intimate pleasure to my spouse. Sexual holiness means I want God to use me for fulfilling my husband/wife. The goal of sexual intimacy is not to receive personal fulfillment, it is to give it. Discuss how to apply this to your marriage.

6. Discuss how to apply this to your love life: "If you want to excel in making love, then seek to do everything you can to please your partner. Learn what he/she likes and do it. Make their pleasure the goal and your pleasure a great by-product of it. Imagine this in action. Both the husband and the wife are doing their absolute best to maximize the experience and pleasure of their partner. I am not trying to have an orgasm. I am seeking to give my wife an incredible experience and an out-worldly orgasm. My goal is for this climax to be the best so far in her life. I promise you, along the road to this my needs will be fully met. Then, if she is doing the same thing, wow! Put this one principle in place in your relationship and lovemaking. Put the needs of the other person first. (Making) Love is not selfish, it does not seek its own."

7. How can proactive and honest communication before, during and after sex improve the experience of you and your partner? How do you feel when it

comes to talking about sex and during sex?

8. Does the idea of praying during sex and/or asking God to help you improve seem strange? Why?

9. The final thing mentioned is to relax and enjoy the journey. You are on this lifelong journey together. Just chill, improve, and grow. Discuss this with your husband/wife. Does sex make you uptight and worried? Why?

Great Sex Part 2

My goal is to help you understand more than the mechanics of sex. I hope to cultivate an appreciation of the overall environment of the home which results in awesome, mind-blowing sex. This is why I cannot over emphasis the first part of this book. Great relationships lead to great sex and great sex leads to great relationships. It starts with the relationship. We need to have an atmosphere of love all day long if we desire to have an act of love at the end of the day. I once read a quote. I cannot remember who said it, but it is accurate. The writer stated, "Sex begins in the kitchen." This is true. Not the act of sex starting on the breakfast table, but the act of love helping prepare dinner and clean together.

We need to improve the moment by moment, minute by minute aspect of our love relationship. These little moments all day long, often lead to incredible moments at night. I believe there are two main areas which lead to constant improvement.

The first area is communication and talking. The more we talk, the more we know and are known. You talk to your best friend about everything. Let me give you an example. It is 1:40 pm. Denise and I are at this moment on a cruise without kids! We are heading back to the mission field and wanted a week of stress-free relaxation before life and ministry slap us in the face. Today, we slept until 10 am. So, in the last three hours we have talked about the Constitution, military, American history, philosophy, news networks' indoctrination, the role of the church in culture, special need children and parents, a tortilla soup recipe, and she just read me twenty funny tweets about parenting toddlers. I just rattled these things off as I am typing. Don't sell them short. We talked about logical thinking and the role it plays in emotional development. We discussed modern spokespeople for evangelical Christianity and how their character does not agree with the message of grace. In other words, they are extremely rude. We discussed the empty hopes of materialism.

Folks, we talk. We talk all the time about everything. In the constant exchange of ideas and opinions, we learn about who we are and who our spouse is. We foster intellectual and emotional depth. When you talk about life, issues, concerns, fears, doubts, goals, hurts, helps, memories and dreams, you are deepening and bonding your love. The result of this constant and serious conversation is a better relationship. A better relationship leads to better lovemaking. This is because what happens in the bedroom is a physical expression of your heart and mind. If your hearts and minds are connected, it results in physical intimacy. You are one and your sexual lives express your one-ness. It also makes it easier to talk about sex and areas of growth in it.

The truth I feel inadequate to communicate is this. Great sex does not come from technique. It arrives in the wake of kindness, thoughtfulness, encouragement, and acts of service. I need to be the type of man who my wife would desire. That man is a Godly one. He is a good one. He is a kind person. He is gentle and helpful. He is humble and generous. My wife loves Jesus, and she is the kind of woman who would love a Christ-like man. I want to be that Jesus following guy she is in love with.

The greatest turn on in a marriage is trust. I would go so far to say trust, honor, service, kindness, thoughtfulness, humility, respect, purity, loyalty, and holiness are far greater aphrodisiacs than anything else. When your spouse knows they are the only one in your heart and on your mind, and they are always in your heart and on your mind, it ignites passion.

Show your husband/wife all day long, in small and large acts of kindness and thoughtfulness, that you love them and are thinking of them. A small note of appreciation, a token gift, or coffee in bed are all easy to do ways to express love. I mentioned coffee in bed. I am blessed to office at home. Over 15 years ago, I made a cappuccino and brought it to Denise in bed to start her day. She appreciated it. I could see it really meant something to her. We talked about it and she said it let her start the day feeling cared for. Since that moment so long ago, I get up and make Denise a special cup of coffee each morning. I drink normal, black, k-cup coffee. Denise likes espresso, cappuccinos, brewed, percolated, and French press coffee. She enjoys a mix. Every morning I make myself a simple, ordinary cup of black coffee and then spend about five minutes whipping her up a cup of love. I have special creamers, syrups, coffees, and equipment. I make her some creation and take it to her. She stays in bed and sips it while I move on with my day. This is an easy-peasy, less than five-minute task for me. It lets her begin each morning with a tangible "I love you".

My point is we cannot make great love unless we love greatly. Love is not that physical ten minutes of sex. It is the 23 hours and 50 minutes preceding that moment. Show your spouse you love them. Small touches and kind words go a long way. Denise and I once read, I believe it was in a book by Gary Smalley, how important a one minute hug is for you emotionally. We give four or five stop-everything-and-relax-in-my-arms one minute hugs a day. We never leave the other without a hug and a kiss. We almost never leave the room without at least a peck on the cheek. These are all physical expressions of heart connectedness. I know she loves me. She knows I love her. What happens in our bedroom is nothing more than an expression of felt love all day long.

Pursue each other romantically. Take the time to date and romance each other. Let love making be the end result of a period of time leading up to it. We go on at least one date a week. This is a tradition which we rarely, pretty much almost never, break. We have been lower middle class to poor most of our marriage because of ministry choices and having a large family. For most of our lives, we did not have disposable income. We still went on a date. We walked in a park for two hours. We shared a glass of tap water at Starbucks. We split a Wendy's 99 cent single burger. We mall walked. We bought an ice-cream and shared it while strolling. Money never stopped us from dating. It limited the expense of the date we could choose, but it did not keep us from choosing to date. Date one another. Pursue the relationship. Men, if you cannot buy flowers, find some wild ones and pick them or plant some and pick them. Write love poems and send small, corny, short videos to each other. One thing I do not understand is why couples stop doing the things which brought them together. When you were dating, you laughed, communicated, played, shared, discovered activities you enjoyed doing together, ate dinner out, went to concerts and plays, tried new hobbies, etc. Why stop it now?

Men, seek to bring romance into your lives. Plan the dates. Book a vacation and plan it out in detail. Choose a nice place to eat. Dress up. I mentioned we are on a cruise. Twice I have overheard women talking and the gist of their conversation was how much they like the dining room because, "We never dress up and go out. I never have an opportunity to wear a nice dress and he never puts on a tie for me." You don't have to dress up all the time, but do it some of the time. Send your wife an e-card or a nice email. Buy flowers every once in a while and remember little things. Let her know she is always on your mind. Speak kind, encouraging, and tender words to her. Be her biggest cheerleader and the one who praises her the most.

Women, remember your husband loves to look at you. Many women will go to great lengths to look good for people at the office, the store, or church, but not do much at home for the man they love. I am not saying you should go all out every day. Denise is beautiful and she rarely, if ever, wears makeup. She doesn't run around the house in skimpy lingerie. However, she takes care of herself and wears clothes she knows I like. Her casual wear for the house is bought with comfort and Joe in mind. Your husband finds pleasure in looking at you. It's okay to dress with him in mind. Another thing your husband wants is to know you love and respect him. So, tell him. Give him words of encouragement. Speak kindly to him. Be specific in your praise, thankfulness, and encouragement.

As you age in your marriage, be intentional on spicing

things up and having fun. Play together. Do not fall into a rut. We were in the States on our furlough and going to be in our Florida home near Orlando for six months. So, we maximized it. We looked up community theater and professional venues and splurged on a couple of nice plays. We watched the comedian Jim Gaffigan perform live. We booked an occasional night at nearby inexpensive hotels. We camp in tents at a state and national parks. We bought Florida resident Disney passes and went to the parks. These are all things from our previous year in the States. I am 59 and she is 56. These are not things only young people with energy and money can do. Please remember, the vast majority of the people who purchase this book make more money than we do. We did these things on a limited budget. You do not have to be young and rich to spend money on enjoying time together. Our goal is not to just go out, it is to go out and have fun as we romance and play together. It doesn't matter how old/young or poor/rich you are, you can discover ways to do new and exciting things together. We just took a break and went to the pool on the ship. They have a 10 story slide called the Abyss. We raced on it twice. We then did the three water slides two times each before going to sit in the hot tub. We did it all together and laughed together doing it. Remember, we are grandparents. Fun doesn't stop with age. Keep pursuing enjoyable pastimes together!

You can spice things up in your bedroom as well. We have purchased several sex board games through the years and played them, until, as my wife put it, "We have to put on our reading glasses to see the card. Kinda kills the moment." :) The joy of getting older. ;) Right now on our bedside table is the book, "A Celebration Of Sex After 50". We are reading it out loud to each other. Denise said we might buy a book of bedroom ideas to check out for fun. Many of those ideas will be out of our comfort zone, but a lot of them will be a new way to enjoy being with each other. Go good old-fashioned 'parking': making out in the car. More than once Denise, after a date, had me pass our driveway where all the littles were at home waiting for us, to go park in the woods and make out in private. I still remember how knowing that she wanted to do that made me loose my stomach. Add some zest to deepen your relationship, and through improving that, you improve your sexual lives as well. Remember the mantra, a great relationship leads to great sex and great sex leads to a great relationship.

Denise and I both try to look good at bedtime. There is a specific type of t-shirt she likes on me. I always wear one of those to bed, along with pajama shorts or pants. I dress up for her and she for me. Every night, when it is time to actually sleep, I take off the shirt. I don't like sleeping in one. She might take off what she has on for something more utilitarian as well. We did not dress to go to bed. We dress to go to bed with our loved one. I want her to be aroused or, at the bare minimum, not turned off by how I look. She has no worries about that with me! The sight of her lights my fire! This is why, as I mentioned earlier, I take a shower every night. We do not have sex every night. Most of the time, we do not make love. I am not dressing for sex. I am seeking to look and smell nice for my wife. I want to be physically attractive to her and she wants to be visually pleasing to me as well. If we do make love, then dressing up the previous three nights was more than worth it!

I stole the following coinage of a word from a source I cannot remember. The truth is, I read a lot. What I read sticks with me. Years later, such as now, when I am writing and a thought comes into my mind, I know is not original, but I do not remember the source. So, if you read this and it was you, let me know and I can give you credit next time. Now to the terminology I referred to:

I counsel couples to spend a lot of time on Othercourse, Outercourse and then Intercourse.

Othercourse is where we should spend most of our time. This is the point of this book. This refers to acts of non-sexual love. It means doing things for your spouse out of a servant's heart. It is doing for them what they like, want, or need done with joy. Denise loves massages. We cannot afford them. In Bolivia I set up a portable table and put blankets on it. I then put on spa music, lit a scented candle, and started a diffuser with essential oils. Earlier I shared the story of the man who gave his wife one massage a week for a year. I did it. We looked at our calendar and scheduled a "one-hour night time massage which will not end in sex" (my words) at least once per week for a year. If a calendar conflict happened, we rescheduled the massage. I bought a book on how to give massages, various muscle groups and techniques. We bought hot stones and good massage oil. We planned ahead while in the States. So, for no less than one hour per week for a year, Denise received an act of love which she knew was not motivated by sexual desire. That is Othercourse. You do acts of love and generosity, service and other-focused actions which have nothing to do with sex. There is no underlying hope or motivation. It is purely,

"I love you and you love this, so I want to do it for you."
Othercourse are those dates and fun activities already
mentioned. It is spending time together and enjoying each
other. Play a game, listen to an audio book, casually pat a
shoulder, do a task in the house they do not like doing, and
other generally unnoticed expressions of love and service.
In my opinion, Othercourse is the most important part of a
marriage and…even though the definition excludes sexual
intent, Othercourse is the greatest producer of awesome sex.
This is because your partner knows you love them. You did
these things out of a pure motivation of selfless love.You
value them. It builds a relationship and…"A great
relationship leads to great sex."

The next activity married people ought to focus on is
Outercourse. Othercourse are expressions of love which
exclude sexual intent. Outercourse is sexual expressions of
love that don't necessarily end in intercourse. Outercourse
is physical. Deep and sensual kissing, touch, cuddling, and
making out are examples of outercourse. Many times
Outercourse leads to someone having an orgasm. It is
providing your partner a climax without actual sexual
penetration. There are many means of doing this.
Outercourse can be a means of fulfilling a sexual desire that
one soulmate has when perhaps the other can not or does
not desire to have full intercourse. This can be various
forms of massage, oral sex, rubbing, or whatever you are
comfortable with. This is another opportunity for open and
honest communication between you two. Many times, one
of us will choose to serve the other person instead of having
intercourse. Often I can provide a much deeper climax to
my wife if I am not as concerned about my own

orgasm...either having one or not having one. Sometimes I will choose to not have sex and instead give her an awesome focused time. She does the same for me. This results in only one of us having a climax, but both of us having a blast. It is also a love deposit for future, greater sex. I place high priority on it as well. The reason is, for many couples, their sex lives become little more than quickies and clean up. They almost never make out. Rarely spend more than a minute kissing. No prolonged time enjoying arousal. It is just a simple, aroused, release, over. Outercourse focuses on arousal and extended arousal with the joy being turned on provides. It says there is more to our physical lives than a quickie. It is enjoying the adventure of sexuality. Sometimes outercourse for one, leads to outercourse for the other and that's good too.

Finally, have a lot of Intercourse. We all know what that means, but also it takes many variations. I have written about this, a lot of it. However, mix it up. Denise and I enjoy going out to eat. There is fast food. This is just a bite to stave off our hunger. Our most often eat out is what we call medium food. Chipotle would be an example. It isn't fast food, but there are no waiters, hostesses or food runners. It takes longer than fast food but less time than a restaurant. The last thing is the restaurant. Those come on the spectrum as well. You can have an average sit down experience or a luxury dining destination.

This is a great way to describe your intercourse. Don't eat fast food every day. Sure, if you just need to get something quick to eat you can go to Taco Bell and sometimes it just hits the spot. But having Taco Bell for every meal wouldn't be a healthy choice for your diet.

Don't let your sexual Intercourse become the equivalent of a fast food place. It's not the most healthy choice for a full and healthy sex life. It is okay to do it often, but come on, not all the time. Then, the the majority of the time you can enjoy good food at a quality price. Medium food. Most of the time in our marriage this is our sexual relationship. We're not in a rush, we are here to enjoy our meal and savor some conversation. Finally, there are the long, sit-down, fancy restaurants. These are take your time and maybe it takes all evening experiences. This is good for your sex life as well. The occasional long, well thought out, enjoy the entire multiple course event before dessert type of sex. You need all of them.

Great Sex Part 2 Reflection Questions

1. Once more we see the emphasis on our relationship outside of the bedroom and how it is the greatest determiner of our sexual fulfillment. Discuss with each other how to improve your moment by moment life together.

2. Joe said, "The greatest turn on in a marriage is trust. I would go so far to say trust, honor, service, kindness, thoughtfulness, humility, respect, purity, loyalty, and holiness are far greater aphrodisiacs than anything else. When your spouse knows that they are the only one in your heart and on your mind, and they are always in your heart and on your mind, it ignites passion. My point is we cannot make great love unless we love greatly. Love is not that physical ten minutes of sex. It is the 24 hours preceding that moment. Show your spouse you love them." What can you do, practically speaking, to let your spouse know they are number one and the only one on your heart and mind?

3. How can you increase and improve the romantic part of your lives? Apart and together plan events focused on increasing intimacy and romance. Schedule them and prioritize them.

4. Discuss with each other things you like and/or desire in your romantic relationship. Start living with the other person in mind.

5. Together plan on how to spice up and improve your non-sexual lives. Things as simple as going on a date to a new place or a fun experience together. What can you do to break out of the routine of life and bring new adventure and fire to it? If you need date ideas there are a myriad of the you can find with a quick internet search.

6. Do the same thing as number five only in the bedroom. How can you break out of the normal sex routine and add spark, spice and excitement to it? Make a plan.

7. Make a plan individually and together to improve your Othercourse. This should be the focus of your relationship. Joe stated in his mind the best way to improve Intercourse is through Othercourse. Put a lot of ideas on paper and schedule them.

8. Learn to incorporate unselfish Outercourse. Focus on doing what your partner likes and providing them with an orgasm in a way other than through Intercourse.

9. Using the idea of going to a restaurant, describe your normal sex life. Is it fast food, medium food, sit down dining or a luxurious meal? How can you incorporate new intercourse avenues? What can you do to avoid a fast food only sexual diet?

One Anothers During Sex

Earlier we spent time looking at the one-anothers in Scripture. These guide our relationships with each other and specifically apply to couples. Once you understand a Biblical worldview of sex, you can see how these apply to making love as well. The married bed is holy and good. Applying relational principles to the act of sex is a wonderful way to improve your love life. This makes perfect sense because sex is the deepest and highest point of relationship expression. It is the illustration of Christ's relationship with the church.

Love one another.

We are to love each other with God's unconditional love. Once we love each other unselfishly throughout the day, it is easier to love unselfishly in the night. Go back to 1 Corinthians 13 where God describes His love. "Love is patient." Patience in sex extends the arousal and excitement phase. It intentionally waits and postpones good in order to experience the best. "Love is kind". Tenderness and kindness expressed in the act of lovemaking elevate it to the next level. Doing something your spouse desires with loving kindness is the heart of lovemaking. "Love does not seek its own." The best sex is unselfish sex. It is when we do not seek our own, but the good of others. My purpose is you and your pleasure, and your purpose is me and my pleasure. Together, our purpose is us and our pleasure.

Be devoted to one another (Romans 12:10).

This means we are to radically focus our attention on the

other person. We concentrate on who they are and what they need. In the act of sex, we are to give our focused attention on the joy and pleasure of our partner. This really is an act of passion, because my passion is you. I am devoted, passionate, about you. you have my focused attention. I want to do everything I can do for you. This time is not about me.

Honor one another above yourselves (Romans 12:10).
The word honor is an idea of respecting someone by elevating them. When you make love, your partner ought to feel your sincere desire to put them above you. Devoted is to be focused on them. Honored is more emotional. They feel it. Lovemaking is not merely physical. It is emotional and in honoring each other, your partner knows you love and respect them in this moment.

Live in harmony with one another and accept one another (Romans 12:16, 15:7).
We are not in competition with each other. Instead, we are in completion with each other. We need to understand the uniqueness and differences of our spouse sexually and then use that knowledge to improve the experience of our loved one. I am to complete Denise in every way. Celebrating our differences allows us to experience the harmony we already spoke about. Generally speaking, men are aroused by sight more than women. This should not irritate the wife because her husband can become instantly excited when she changes into her pajamas in front of him. She should accept it and use it for sexual enjoyment on his behalf. Men, your wife wants tenderness, gentleness, time,

and thoughtful words. Do not be upset if she is not instantly aroused after a long and tiring day. Instead, make it your goal to slowly stimulate her. She needs conversation and focus. Talk to her. Let her unwind and warm up. The fact she takes a little longer allows you to enjoy arousal as well. Enjoy the fact you are different and do not try to change each other. Instead, do what the other person enjoys. The fact they like it, even if it is not the same thing as what you enjoy, is why you do it.

Build up one another (Romans 14:19; 1 Thessalonians 5:11).

Our words and actions are who we are. Our words ought to improve the heart and emotions of our spouse. This is true in bed as well. Complement and speak kindly to your spouse during sex. Brag on their ability to please you. Let them know how much you love and desire them. In the Bible, the Song of Solomon is full of intimate speech. Use it as your model. Talk to your spouse intimately. Compliment their body. Look into their eyes and speak life to them. Sex is far more than a physical event. It is an emotional connection. Build your spouse up before, during, and after intercourse.

Care for one another (1 Corinthians 12:25, Ephesians 4:32).

Caring for each other is basically considerate actions of love. It is showing kindness and concern through thoughtful actions and gentle words. The sexual applications of this verse are exponential. It ought to describe sex. Loving, caring, and gentle. Your sexual life is a means of expressing your care.

Serve one another. Be kind and compassionate to one another (Galatians 5:13).

Caring for each other is meeting needs. This goes one step beyond that. You don't just seek to meet needs; you search for ways to express love by giving your spouse thoughtful service. I believe this is one of the key components of great sex. When your goal is self satisfaction, your spouse can feel used. When you are really serving them, they know it. They experience your desire to serve and bless them in the highest form of intimacy.

Submit to one another (Ephesians 5:21, 1 Peter 5:5).

This is the twin of honoring the other. When I honor you, I lift you up as more important than myself. Submission is joyfully submitting my will to you. You are not submitting if your submission was your desire all along. Submission is "doing the will of my authority with the same joy and attitude as my own will. It is doing what I don't want to do with the passion of my own personal choice." It is not begrudging giving in to them. It is joyfully allowing them the choice. This is best seen when one partner desires sex and the other does not. The one who does will not even know the other partner wasn't in the mood if real submission happens. My wife submitted her desire to go to sleep 20 minutes sooner to my desire to make love, and I did not even know it happened. I thought she was more aroused then me. We joyfully surrender our will and our rights to the service of the marriage and the other. It is never done with a pout. It is always a joy.

One Anothers During Sex Reflection Questions

1. This is a straightforward chapter with deep repercussions. Go over each of these one-anothers and ask your partner how you can best do this for them during the act of making love. Give your spouse no less than two applications per point.

   a) Love
   b) Devotion
   c) Honor
   d) Harmony
   e) Edify
   f) Likeminded
   g) Accept
   h) Care
   i) Serve
   j) Kind
   k) Submit
   l) Pray

FAQ'S

What is the ideal frequency for sex?

This is pretty straightforward. You should have sex as often as each person wants it. There is no formula. My wife makes love to me when I want to make love. I make love to her as often as she desires. We do not need to compare ourselves with others and see how we measure. Our sexual intimacy is a private event. However, the point of this book is you should have a lot of sex. Anytime your spouse initiates sex, have it. Go back to "why not?" Denise once told a group of women during a retreat, "Why would I not do something that is so easy and quick to do yet means so much to him?" Honestly, saying no does far more harm than most people think, and saying yes takes so little effort and results in an orgasm, contentment, deeper relationships and happiness. If you think he/she wants to do it too much, you are probably doing it too little. My limited research and practical experience through ministry says this. Adults, through 30 years, have sex twice a week. 30-50 have sex twice a month. 50-60 have it once every three weeks. 60+ once a month declining as physical ability diminishes. My goal has always been to be an overachiever! The main thing to look for is simple. Are both people truly and honestly satisfied with the frequency of your sexual life?

How do we increase frequency?

The main way is to deepen intimacy and love outside of the bedroom. I said earlier, "You will not make great love until you love greatly." True lovemaking is an extension of felt love. It is the 23 hours leading up to sex which lead to sex. The best way to increase your sexual life is to improve your non-sexual one. Another way is to manage your stress and rest. It is difficult to look forward to the night if you dread your day. Sex is not compartmentalized. Your life is not in boxes. It is holistic. Learn to manage life. Decrease your stress. Add margin. Enjoy noontime and you will enjoy nighttime. However, in all honesty, the best way to increase frequency is to have sex. Just. Do. It. The more you have sex, the more sex you will want to have. Do not wait for the perfect time. Make this moment the perfect time and make love. Finally, for more mature or longer married couples, spice up your sexual lives through intentional activities. You can find so many ideas in books and on-line. Make your bedroom your playground. One easy practical idea is if one or both of you have long and tiring days that make it difficult to have sex in the evening, then set your clock and get up a little earlier and enjoy it in the morning. Don't just 'skip' it.

What constitutes 'Good Sex'?

This is another personal answer. One thing we stress in counseling is, with very rare exception, sex doesn't end until both people experience orgasm and contentment. Other than that, a basic formula for thinking this through is: Anticipation, Arousal, Excitement, Culmination, Contentment.

Anticipation is part of the romantic and outside of the bedroom experience. It is knowing sex is going to happen. It might be a romantic getaway or a phone call to the office promising it. In some manner, you know tonight is the night. I personally enjoy thinking about it all day long.

Sometimes Denise will gift me with the knowledge that tonight she plans on taking her time with me. My entire day is looking forward to the night. The anticipation is fun.

Arousal is the initial phase and includes hugging, kissing, looking, intimate talk, and physical contact. It initiates the physical responses of the body of both man and woman. This is the real beginning point. Unfortunately, this point is often barely touched upon. It is like excitement in the next point. Couples, especially after being married a while and having children, tend to try and go from nothing to orgasm as quickly as possible. This is satisfying, but not nearly as much as spending time in arousal and excitement.

Excitement is the phase most often skipped by couples who have been together for a while. Excitement is the point after arousal and before actual orgasm. Great sex extends this time period. Studies reveal, and this is especially true as one gets older, that extending the excitement phase to at least ten minutes produces a much stronger orgasm. The excitement phase is where self-control and other orientation are best seen. This is because the more, and longer, you are in this phase, everything in you is pushing you to move to the last phase. Your body is screaming at you to move on to culmination. Be intentional and increase this stage long as you can.

Culmination is self-explanatory. Outercourse can be an orgasm gift, but intercourse should always end in both people climaxing in orgasm. Both people have at least one. If one person has an orgasm and cannot continue the act of intercourse, they should lovingly serve their spouse in another way to give an orgasm. The last point is contentment. Sex isn't over until both of you are totally satisfied with the experience and enjoy some time talking and cuddling in the cool down phase.

What is 'Off Limits' in sex?

There are two overarching principles to guide this. Before I give them, let me first say anything that leads to lustful thinking, fantasizing outside of your marriage, or involving in any form another person is sin. This includes pornography. Making love is an intimate expression of holy love between a man and a wife. Period. Nothing else physical, mental, or emotional is allowed by God. It is immoral and sinful. Now, the principles. First, each person must be consensual and agreeable to everything which happens in the marriage bed. The activity is other oriented and designed to express love. Second, no part of the body is clean and another dirty. When God created the first couple, He explicitly stated, "They were naked and unashamed." There is no shame in your body. Your ear is not clean, but your penis nasty. Your vagina is not shameful, but your elbow holy. Your body is one thing, and it is good. There are aspects of your body the Bible exclusively limits to your marriage bed. That does not make those parts of your body shameful. It means they are holy for a specific use. Therefore, what a couple decides to do, which involves only the two of them physically, emotionally, and mentally, is acceptable when both agree to it. Oral sex, hand stimulation, rubbing on each other, and multiple positions are not off limits. Decide together what you like, what you want to try, where your limits are placed.

It hurts when we make love (typically women).

This is physical and might need to involve a physician. It could be something as easily solved as applying lubrication. We recommend to couples to use lubricant freely, try multiple positions and angles and let the woman control the depth, speed and intensity of thrusting. Talk throughout the event in order to identify specific pain triggers. If you cannot find and eliminate the pain on your own, then go to a doctor. Sex is to be mutually enjoyable and if it isn't, identify and solve the problem.

It is hard to enjoy sex because of shame and guilt of sexual choices in my past.

This is a normal problem with an easy supernatural solution. Go to the cross and receive forgiveness and, by faith, believe it. Your past behavior and sexual sin are forgiven and erased. Now, by faith, believe sex is holy and good. Satan will constantly attack you on this front in order to destroy the beauty of holy intercourse. Walk, and make love, by faith. God has forgiven you and gifted you with this beautiful thing we call sex. It is a good gift from Him and glorifies Him.

I don't really desire sex.

This is one of the reasons for this book. A lack of desire stems from either a poor worldview of sex or a weak relationship. Sexual desire flows from an awesome relationship. It also leads to one. By faith, have sex anytime your spouse desires it, knowing it is good and holy. Outside of the bedroom, seek to improve and deepen your relationship. If you do this and still have a low libido, it is most likely hormonal and easy for a doctor to help through medication. Many times over-the-counter supplements can help.

I struggle with premature ejaculation.

This is a normal occurrence, especially early in marriage. The key to this is two-fold. Learn, through practice, to identify the moment before you ejaculate. Pray and seek self-control and stop the stimulation before. Your goal is to give her an orgasm. Keep that goal in mind. Withdraw from her and stimulate her another way until you are under control again. Practice and practice until you know your limit and you stop on time to extend the event. There are activities and things you can do to help with this. Look them up and do them together until you have victory.

I struggle with physical intimacy and sex after sexual assault and trauma.

Again, sexual assault and trauma are way to frequent in the world and we understand that many readers of our book have experienced ugliness and evil of it. If you are continuing to struggle in your sex life with your spouse after experiencing sexual assault or trauma in your past, you are not alone and you don't have to try and heal alone.

"The Lord is close to the brokenhearted and saves those who are crushed in spirit." Psalm 34:18

Recovering from sexual assault takes time, and the healing process can be painful. You can regain your sense of control, rebuild your self-worth, and heal. Regardless of age or gender, the impact of sexual violence goes far beyond any physical injuries. The trauma of being raped or sexually assaulted can be shattering, leaving you feeling scared, ashamed, and alone. You might have flashbacks or other unpleasant memories. You might not feel safe anywhere. You no longer trust others. Again, you are not alone and you as a couple do not have to walk through the healing process alone. We will share some practical guidelines that might help, but we again say that most likely you could greatly benefit from talking to a specialist about this. Talking to a Christian professional who is trained to help heal these long lasting wounds is well worth the cost. Don't let satan gain an ongoing victory by keeping you miserable and in pain. You were the victim of a hideous crime, don't let that steal your future of tender, meaningful, and enjoyable love making. There is hope. Seek out that hope until you find it.

Here is a quick list of practical helps to start:

- First off, and we cannot emphasize this too much, forgive the one(s) who hurt you. This is for your healing.
- Identify your specific triggers and boundaries to understand what your healing process should work to address.
- Move at your own pace give yourself time and be gentle with yourself. Your spouse should treat you with the utmost tenderness as well.
- Test out different coping mechanisms for trauma healing such as talk therapy, mindfulness, and don't be afraid to use medication as needed.

- Re-associate intimacy, touch, and sensuality with positive connotations.
- Be in constant communication with your spouse.

I do not experience an orgasm.

This could be hormonal. More than once in couples we have counseled, the culprit has been birth control pills. We advised them to use another form of control and once the hormones from the pill left their system, they could have an orgasm. If it isn't hormonal, then it could be technique. Relax and be tender as you stimulate your wife or your husband. There is no time limit. Talk to each other and identify actions and areas which feel better. Keep it going with slow, relaxed, tender, and loving communication until we, not just me, have an orgasm. Do this every time. Once more, practice, practice and practice some more. Sometime orgasms tend to fade away if we are trying too hard on concentrating on them too much. Just relax and enjoy the time. While keeping the goal of an orgasm, try to just give in fully to the journey without the the serious pressure of the ending. Also, there are lots of experts out there who can help with this. Don't be embarrassed to seek help from a professional therapist. It could literally change your life.

Remember, sex is not an event. Sex is a journey of love and togetherness. It is an expression of love. It is an area of growth. Read biblically sound books on sex. There are thousands of resources a click away on the internet. Read books out loud to each other in bed. Play games in bed. Do things to enjoy and expand your sexual life. Sex is a vital part of a marriage relationship, if you can't seem to get to where you want to be in this aspect of your relationship on your own, please seek out a professional to help you. Any time and money put into improving your sexual relationship is money well invested.

Made in the USA
Columbia, SC
18 June 2024

36768415R00117